To Manoj
A million thanks
— Paul.

ASYLUM
Paul Kember

Warner Chappell Plays

LONDON

 A Warner Communications Company

First published in 1989
by Warner Chappell Plays Ltd.,
129 Park Street, London W1Y 3FA.

ISBN 0 85676 140 0

Typeset and printed by Commercial Colour Press, London E7.
Cover design by Helen Lannaghan.
Photo of Paul Kember by Geoff Shields

ASYLUM was first presented at the Belgrade Theatre Coventry, on 11th October 1988 with the following cast:

TILLY	Sarah Miles
FLO	Ann Way
TERRY	Ian Collier
GEORGIE	Michael O'Hagan
ROGER	Peter Attard
JOK	David Fenwick
LUKE	Philip Lowrie
DICK	Peter Sproule

Director Rob Walker
Designer Stewart Laing
Lighting Designer Kevin Sleep

The Belgrade Theatre production subsequently transferred to the Lyric Theatre Hammersmith, London, on 8th November 1988.

To my mother and father,
Peggy and John

Characters

TILLY — Late forties, early fifties; an ex-long-stay personality-disordered patient; liable to fly off the handle at any moment; resourceful; nobody's fool.

DICK — Late forties, early fifties; a tacky, not very successful pop video producer. Sympathetic and a good heart but insensitive at times. Always tries to do the best for others, but the world conspires to thwart him more often than he'd like to admit.

FLO — Early sixties; a long-stay schizophrenic patient. Institutionalised. Not very stable.

ROGER — Late twenties; a first-assistant. Pragmatic, follows his nose.

LUKE — Late twenties. A pop video director. Convinced of his own talent. Hard-working but just hasn't got it.

TERRY — Late forties. An occasional patient, manic-depressive. Upright, an ex-military man. Once had a promising career in the City. Now an estate-agent.

GEORGIE — Late forties. A committed, sympathetic, kindly nurse.

JOK — Early twenties. A second-rate pop hopeful.

ACT ONE

Scene One

The huge, landscaped gardens of a nineteenth-century lunatic asylum.

A large oak tree. Under its shade, a park bench.

Nearby, a large statue of Lord Shaftesbury.

Birds sing. Tranquil country sounds.

At the back of the stage, a large solid wall with an ornamental gate. The gate is heavily padlocked.

Leaning against the wall is an old grass roller. Next to it, an ancient tractor furrow blade.

Sitting under the tree, on the bench, is FLO.

ROGER *enters with a canvas film chair. He sets it down and exits.*

DICK *enters from the opposite direction, carrying a large brass victorian dedication plaque. On it is a large lot number and a red 'sold' label.*

Music plays. A turgid, modern pop song. DICK *looks offstage and shouts:*

DICK	Cut that row!
ROGER	(*off*) What?
DICK	I said, knock that racket off! (*He mimes cutting his own throat. The music snaps off.*) That's better. I haven't had my breakfast yet.
	(*He takes out a handkerchief. Wipes the plaque and blows away the dust. He reads out the inscription.*)
	"In memory of Doctor Elias Shadwell ... in gratitude for his untiring zeal ... and unselfish devotion ... to the sick ... and distressed of the borough."
	(*He straightens up.*)
	Nice. (*To* FLO.) That'll look very nice in my new conservatory.

(ROGER *enters, with staff nurse* GEORGIE
following. DICK *puts the plaque to one side.*)

Ah, Staff Nurse Ingle, I presume?

GEORGIE   That's correct. You must be Mr Headley?

DICK   Dick Headley's the name, pop promos are
the game. Nice to meet you, I'm sure we're
gonna have a lot of fun together. (*They shake
hands.*) You've met my personal assistant,
Roger, the number-two-chief?

ROGER   That's very nice of you, Guv'nor.

(DICK *puts his arm around* GEORGIE *and walks
him forward.*)

DICK   Now Roger and I are called Bootstrap
Productions ...

ROGER   Catchy. Very.

DICK   Every little pop movie we make is important
to us. Each one gets us the next job. And if
just one goes up the spout, so does the
company. Now that can make us very tense.
Right, Roger?

ROGER   Like piano wire.

DICK   On the other hand, if things go well for us,
we can be very happy. Is *that* not a fact, Rog?

ROGER   Fact, not fiction. We can be delirious.

DICK   See, we're hoping this could be the one that
comes down the line with 'gravy-train' written
on the side. The big one that takes our little
company out of the shadow of bankruptcy
and into the land of fame and plenty. And if
that happens, there's a pint in it for you.

GEORGIE   That's very kind of you.

DICK   Danger is, in a place like this, it could go the
other way. The whole bloody thing could
come right off the rails. And that would be a
disaster.

ROGER   Total disaster.

               (LUKE *enters, making notes on his shooting script.*)

DICK   Now, Staff, I like to be "commodious" with
               the people I work with. I don't like anything
               "portentious". I'm an off-the-shoulder, shoot-
               from-the-hip kind of guy. And I know you'll
               understand me when I say that if you have
               any nice-looking girls hanging around, let
               'em roam free. That kind of person always
               looks nice in the shot as a bit of set
               decoration. You get me?

GEORGIE   (*uneasy*) Well, this is hardly the place . . .

DICK   That's one thing. The other is: some of the
               brothers and sisters here may, not to put too
               fine a point on it, go a bit loopy. They may
               decide to attack us in a fit of "pick".

               (FLO *exits.*)

               Or somesuch and various. The possibilities
               are endless. Now I'd like an assurance from
               you that if you have any "incontinentals" or
               dribblers, perverts, head-bangers, wild-boys
               and so on, you'll keep 'em in check and out
               of our way.

GEORGIE   Nothing is going to happen, I can assure
               you.

               (LUKE *enters. He has a camera around his neck.
               He takes photographs of the statue and gardens.*)

DICK   Good. That's what I wanted to hear because
               if anything untoward *should* happen, I want
               you to know that I shall have the balls of the
               person or persons concerned — and I shall
               have them boiled in oil. I hope I make myself
               clear.

GEORGIE   Everyone has been told to be on their best
               behaviour. Now, if you'll excuse me, I've got
               work to do . . .

(GEORGIE *exits.* JOK *enters, coat slung over his shoulder, images of Frank Sinatra running through his mind. He looks around.*)

DICK   (*shouting after him*) Good. That makes me happy.

ROGER   (*ditto*) That makes *me* delirious!

DICK   (*as he exits*) He gonna be all right, d'you think?

ROGER   Yeah, he got the message.

(*They exit.* JOK *strolls over to* LUKE. *He is brimming with confidence.*)

JOK   Well?

LUKE   Well, what?

JOK   How was I in the rehearsal, then? Good? Brilliant? Don't tell me I was *better* than brilliant?

LUKE   Yeah. Fine.

JOK   Oh. Great. Thanks a bunch.

(*He walks away, disappointed. He stops, turns to* LUKE.)

You know I've always thought *I* should be in a place like this.

LUKE   (*not in the least interested*) Oh, really? Why's that?

JOK   (*full of pride*) Because I'm a bloody madman, *me*. Totally crazy.

(*He swaggers off.* ROGER *enters, making notes on a clipboard.*)

LUKE   The pop video is one notch up on the porno film. Did you know that, Roger?

ROGER   If you say so, Guv.

LUKE   Anyone can make a pop video. But to do it *well* calls for something special. Nine out of ten are dross. The tenth is inspired. I make only tens. And this is gonna be another. It's gonna be tough, it's gonna be uncompromising. It's gonna be *me*.

ROGER   You want a bacon sandwich, Guv'nor?

LUKE   This film will talk to people. It'll be relevant. It'll be "*now*".

ROGER   Or kippers. I think they've got kippers on.

LUKE   The skid is to make *your* films while making them think you're making *their* films. These pop singers . . . they're just camera-frightened amateurs, even the biggest of them. They see the lens, they go weak. And that's my strength. I articulate for them what they cannot articulate for themselves.

ROGER   You said it, Guv'nor.

LUKE   I'm not interested in rock 'n' roll. I'm interested in life. When this monstrosity is torn down and just a bad memory, we'll have a record of what it was like. I'm going to capture it in all its hideous, sick grandeur. I shall bear witness and my footage will be my testimony. I've wanted to get inside here for years to make a statement. To capture this insult to human dignity. This abattoir of the spirit. I know these people, these inmates.

(FLO *enters. They watch her.*)

They're soul-brothers and soul-sisters. I know their feeling of fear; of hanging on to your reality. It's a country I've lived in. Are you ready to be inspired, Roger?

ROGER   Whatever you say, Guv'nor.

LUKE   Let's get it in the can, kid. Let's make images.

(*He slaps* ROGER *on the back.*)

ROGER   Yes, Guv.

(ROGER *exits and* LUKE *carries on taking photos.* FLO *walks into his field of vision.*)

LUKE   Excuse me. Could you just move a little to
            the left? I want to get the tower in.

FLO   What are you doing?

            (*Suddenly,* LUKE *looks out from behind his
            camera.*)

LUKE   Oh, what a great face. Like a Bruegel. (*He
            offers his hand to* FLO.) The name's Luke. I'm
            gonna be here for the day.

            (*She ignores it and sits on the bench.*)

FLO   That's nice. I've been here twenty-two years.

            (LUKE *continues to take photographs of her, while
            the sound of heavy plant machinery going about its
            work is heard in the background. Suddenly, a
            plastic bag thuds onto the ground, thrown over the
            wall.*)

FLO   (*going to it*) Where did that come from?

LUKE   (*looking through his lens*) Oh, that's just the
            bulldozers, love.

FLO   No, this.

            (FLO *picks up the bag. She takes out a blouse,
            holds it up against herself.*)

            Nice. Oh, if only there was a skirt to match.

            (*Another bag lands on the ground.* FLO *goes to it
            and takes out a skirt. She looks up to the skies.*)

            Oh, thank you, God!

            (*A head pops up, over the wall. Dressed in the
            clothes of a 'bag-lady', a shower-cap on her head.
            This is* TILLY.)

TILLY   It's me.

FLO   Did you hear something?

TILLY   I'm coming in.

            (FLO *rushes forward, perturbed.*)

FLO	Hey! You can't come in here.
TILLY	I'm coming over.
FLO	No — that wall's to stop people getting in. Go now, hoppit!
TILLY	I'm coming in, don't try to stop me.
	(TILLY *struggles to bring over a pram.*)
LUKE	Sensational!
FLO	No, you can't. This is private property.
TILLY	Can someone help me, please?
FLO	Stop her, someone. She must be mad. Call someone in authority. Georgie! We can't have this.
TILLY	Shut up. Leave me alone. Can someone give me a hand, please? With my pram?
	(LUKE *steps forward to help* TILLY.)
FLO	All hell will break loose. Make her see reason.
LUKE	Jesus. Crazy. Off the wall.
FLO	You can't come in here.
TILLY	Will you shut up, you'll get me into trouble.
	(TILLY *comes forward and removes her hat.*)
FLO	Oh, blimey. I don't believe it. It's . . .
TILLY	Don't tell me you've forgotten me?
FLO	Tilly. Tilly Armitage.
TILLY	That's it. I've absconded, Flo.
FLO	You what?
TILLY	I didn't like living at the seaside. So I've come back. To rejoin my friends.
FLO	But you're supposed to be back in the community.

TILLY	(*walking around, looking at the place*) *This* is my community. I'm back where I belong ... I'm over the moon. (*Seeing* LUKE *crouching, taking photographs*.) He's new! I'm home.
FLO	But there's nowhere for you to stay. They're tearing the place down. Selling it off, bit by bit.
LUKE	(*taking one final picture*) Fabulous, girls. I love it. Wow!
	(LUKE *exits. Suddenly, loud music blurts out.* TILLY *looks up, terrified. Then just as suddenly, it stops.*)
TILLY	What was that?
FLO	Music, I think.
TILLY	Didn't sound like music.
FLO	I know. They're making a pop film or something.
TILLY	Oh, how exciting. In here? What for?
FLO	Ooh, now you've got me. They did explain it to us. We all got a little leaflet. We're not to get in the way and we're to treat them as normal.
TILLY	Sort of occupational therapy, is it?
FLO	Oh no, it's not for our benefit. At least I don't think so. It happens all the time now. They hire the place out, for weddings and twenty-firsts and so forth.
TILLY	But that's crazy.
FLO	Seems to be, yes.
	(TERRY *enters, highly agitated.*)
TILLY	Hello, Terry, remember me? Tilly?
TERRY	(*speaking in order to avoid contact*) I could have been in the French Resistance in the last war,

you know. Only reason I wasn't was because I didn't have the qualifications. One, I wasn't in France. And two — I wasn't even born.

(*He walks away from* TILLY.)

TILLY   How are you, Terry?

TERRY   Did you know that my parents were the most attractive people in the Roaring Twenties? And my father had a penchant for check trousers?

(TERRY *tries the gate to get out.* GEORGIE *enters. He sees* TILLY.)

TILLY   Hello, Georgie. You're still here, then?

GEORGIE   (*surprised*) Tilly? Mathilda Armitage? What are you doing here?

TILLY   I've come back, Georgie.

GEORGIE   Ah, to see all your old friends again? That's nice.

TILLY   No, I've come back to stay. (*She sits on the bench.*)

GEORGIE   *Stay*? They're knocking the place down, my love.

TILLY   But I've nowhere else to go.

GEORGIE   Shaftesbury Ward is gone, my angel.

TILLY   I can't stick it out there.

(GEORGIE *sits next to her.* TERRY *exits.*)

GEORGIE   Ah, how have you been keeping? Not too well?

TILLY   Not too well at all, Georgie.

GEORGIE   Ah, that's too bad. Look — come to my office. We'll have a nice cup of tea and a chat. Come on.

FLO   Oh, a cup of tea would be very welcome. (*As
             they exit.*) Oh, Tilly, I'd like to talk to you
             about this skirt ...

             (*They all exit.* ROGER *enters carrying* DICK'S
             breakfast on a tray. He sets up a table and chair.
             DICK *enters.*)

DICK   You know, Roger, old chap, it's when I see a
             place like this that I thank God I'm normal.

ROGER   I know what you mean, Guv'nor.

DICK   The people who built this place must have
             been mad themselves. If you weren't bonkers
             when you came in here, tramping those
             bloody corridors would drive you off your
             chump. Eh?

ROGER   Hell of a length.

             (DICK *sits.* ROGER *puts a napkin across his knee,
             hands him a knife and fork, takes a cup of tea from
             the tray and sits, sipping it through the following.*)

DICK   Look at these grounds. Land stretching as far
             as the eye can see. Sitting plum in the middle
             of one of the major cities of the world. And
             what's it used for? Just so's a lot of do-lally
             merchants can frolic around and stretch their
             legs. Now if that isn't insane, you tell me
             what is.

ROGER   Mad. Totally.

DICK   God Almighty, what I could have done with
             this land. I could have cleaned up.
             Unfortunately some other bugger thought of
             it before me. Gonna turn it a housing
             estate for first-time buyers and newly-weds.

ROGER   Smart move. Very.

DICK   Course, when they built this place, middle of
             the nineteenth century, this was the outskirts
             of the city, you know?

ROGER   Nah?

DICK   Yeah, the city hadn't come up this far, then.
            This was the whole point. Stick these places
            as far out of civilisations's way as possible.
            Keep the normal and the abnormal members
            of society apart. A sort of "Goo-ga archie-
            pelago".

ROGER   Very wise.

DICK   See, out in the wilderness here, your oafs,
            your dim-wits and your Gormless-Joes could
            be as mad as they liked. And normal people
            like us could live in peace.

ROGER   Probably very nice for 'em to be in the
            country and be able to let off a bit of mad
            steam now and again.

DICK   As you say, Roger. But ... this was the crazy
            part — once you got in here, you bloody-well
            never got out again.

ROGER   Frightening. Very.

DICK   And you could be as sane as you and I, Rog.
            But after a few years of mixing with this sort,
            you ended up as mad as a hatter, too. So
            someone who was put away for, say, stealing
            a bit of bread or falling behind with their
            rent — and you know what a lot of mad
            bastards they were in the old days, they'd
            lock you up for anything — that person
            would become a lunatic, just by being here.
            These places manufactured lunatics; on the
            premises. And this is why they have to be
            knocked down. They're the last "vestible" of a
            barbaric world which now, thank God, is
            coming under the hammer.

            (TERRY *enters, highly agitated.*)

TERRY   Any chance of a sandwich?

DICK	I don't think we've got surplus to our requirements, old son.
TERRY	Bit of spam would go down nice. Or a piece of chicken breast. That'd be a treat. They don't feed us very well here.

(DICK *carries on eating.*)

DICK	Certainly, see what we can do later. Roger, make a note.
ROGER	(*doing nothing*) Note made.
TERRY	Much obliged.

(TERRY *takes out a handful of coins from his pocket and offers them to* DICK.)

I can lend you a couple of bob if you're broke. Give it me back when you're flush.

DICK	That's very considerate, old chap, but I'm fine and dandy at the moment, thank you.
TERRY	Okay. Just give me a shout, ever you need a touch. (*He puts the money away.*)
DICK	Will do. Much obliged.

(DICK *smiles at* TERRY, *obviously wanting to be rid of him.*)

TERRY	I'm getting married tomorrow and I'm off to America to start a new life!
DICK	Oh, lovely.
TERRY	I want a double room somewhere. It's no fun being here. I want a double room in Mayfair, actually, and I want to see my wife.

(TERRY *moves towards* ROGER, *who jumps back.*)

ROGER	Don't you come near me.
TERRY	(*to* DICK) Most of my best friends are French. Did you know that?
DICK	No, I had no idea.

TERRY	I've always tried to keep French friends. I haven't been to Paris for a while, of course. Last time I was there, I found myself in desperate straits, actually. Touch of the old "la plume de ma tante est sur le bureau de mon oncle".
DICK	(*nodding, humouring him*) I know exactly what you mean.
TERRY	I was in a tricky situation, owing to the fact that: one, I had no plume; two, I had no uncles or even an aunt in Paris at that time, and three: I certainly had nothing that in any way resembled a bureau. So you can imagine, I was devastated.
DICK	Well, you would be.
TERRY	(*quiet, almost introspective*) Well, I'd better get going. Going? I've gone already. (*He exits.*)
DICK	Sad, isn't it? He's probably been in here most of his adult life. What a waste.
ROGER	I thought there was gonna be a bit of bother there. I was getting ready to thump him one.
DICK	Don't worry. Nowadays they give these "mind-boggling" drugs. Makes 'em harmless. They just walk around dopey. That's why they call them "miracle" drugs. It's a miracle you can keep so many people so dopey so much of the time. (*Having finished his breakfast, he gets up and re-lights his cigar.*) That's just one of the wonderful strides they've made in the field of psychiatry in recent years. Now you drug 'em up and they can walk around anywhere they like. And the marvellous thing is, they always come back for their tea.
ROGER	Amazing.
DICK	Even go on Spanish holidays, some of the luckier ones.

ROGER   No?

DICK   Yeah. They give 'em a jab in the arse and it
             stops 'em going haywire. You know, talking
             to street-lamps and that. I tell you, the
             modern world ... never ceases to make me
             feel proud. Hundred years ago, all we could
             do was chain 'em to the walls and bore holes
             in their heads, but now look — Spanish
             holidays.

ROGER   Unbelievable. Really.

DICK   The bad old days are gone forever, thank
             God.

ROGER   How d'you know all this? You had a history
             of mental illness in your family, or what?

DICK   (*deeply offended*) Piss off. What a thing to say,
             you berk.

ROGER   Oh. Sorry—

DICK   (*as though this explained everything*) I was in the
             Navy, wasn't I?

             (*Pause.*)

ROGER   Oh. Sorry, Guv'nor, I didn't realise.

DICK   What a prat. What were you trying to imply?

ROGER   Nothing, Guv. No offence intended.

DICK   You got madness in *your* blood?

ROGER   (*irritated now*) Here, knock it off! I'm a
             hundred-per-cent normal, me. We've never
             had anything like that in our family. Not a
             whiff of it. Not a *sniff*, thank you very much.

DICK   Well same here, you berk. There's nobody in
             my family low on the cocoa.

ROGER   All right, all right — I'm sorry!

DICK   I should think so an' all, you mad bastard.

(Pause. DICK looks at ROGER suspiciously. LUKE enters, checking camera positions on his shooting script. DICK sees him and motions to ROGER to exit. ROGER goes. DICK sidles over to LUKE. He looks around to make sure nobody is listening.)

Luke ... I just want to "riterate", before we start the shoot, how thrilled and honoured I am that you're working on my team.

LUKE   You're paying me a lot of money.

DICK   Right. That's because I'm a great admirer of your work. Your "oov-rer". *(He mispronounces 'oeuvre'.)*

LUKE   Thank you.

DICK   And your "moddus operandy".

LUKE   Sorry?

DICK   I'm saying: I've been around the ball-park once or twice myself. I know where the lines are and I know where the goal is. And I know how to get the ball in the net. You get me?

LUKE   Some kind of football analogy?

DICK   I'm saying ... I know the ropes. This Jok, he's a talentless piece of bum-fluff. Am I right?

LUKE   Is a frog's arse watertight?

DICK   Take any artiste in the pop business today. It's not talent that gets them into the charts. It's packaging.

LUKE   That's right.

DICK   We're in a competitive field. Pull something out of the hat for me. Something a little bit *special* to arrest the attention. You get my drift?

LUKE   I don't think I do.

DICK   Luke ... come on, old son. I could have got
                any tuppence-ha'penny mediocrity to direct
                this little movie and pocketed the difference.
                But, this time, I didn't ... I got you. I was
                willing to pay the best to get the best.

LUKE   Thank you.

DICK   Because I expect certain results. I trust I'm
                coming over loud and clear?

LUKE   Perhaps if you employed a little *more*
                clarity ...

DICK   (*moving in closer to* LUKE, *conspiratorially*)
                Look, that bunch of pansies who call
                themselves a band — Dead
                Astronauts ... you made them look like the
                most exciting thing on the pop scene today;
                when, let's face it, we all know they're the
                pits.

LUKE   They really are.

DICK   Those shirt-lifters got to number one because
                of your brilliance with the visuals. Your
                genius, if that's not too weak a word.

LUKE   (*accepting it*) No. That's okay.

DICK   That song had nothing going for it. But once
                they banned the video, it shot straight to
                number one. They shifted two million units
                in this country alone. Even the Pope tried to
                see a copy so's he could ban it, too. You see
                what I'm driving at, Luke?

LUKE   The fact that it was banned was purely
                accidental.

DICK   Of course it was. Course it was. Of *course*. But
                it was a *happy* accident that someone rang the
                BBC and told them that the "ambigwos"
                how's-your-father in the shadows was actually
                two men bonking. Eh? A *very* happy accident
                — and marvellous for business. They got a

big hit and the company that made the video
was inundated with work. Now I leave the
nitty-gritty up to you, but, remember:
copulating couples, that's always a good one.
Get Mary Whitehouse upset. Let's get the
Pope involved — he's very big money these
days. Give me one of your special ones ...
and you could end up with a lot of lolly in
your handbag.

LUKE   You'll get what you paid for. (*He exits.*)

DICK   (*shouting after him*) Good. Then I know we're
on the same wavelength!

(DICK *puffs at his cigar. Offstage, the sound of a
bulldozer being started and a demolition ball
smashing into the nearby buildings.*)

(*Quick fade, as the music plays.*)

Scene Two

*The gardens, an hour or so later, now littered with
the paraphernalia of film-making — cables,
electricity boxes, camera stands, a ladder, paints,
brushes, bits of wood and scaffold, etc. but no
camera.*

As the lights come up, FLO *is sitting on the bench,
knitting. After a moment* TILLY *enters, now
dressed in indoor clothes. She goes over to* FLO.

TILLY   What you making?

FLO   A little cardie, for my Lilly's youngest.

(FLO *holds up the bodice of a little cardigan.*
TILLY *takes it and holds it in front of herself.*)

TILLY   (*suddenly thoughtful*) Oh, dear ...

FLO   What's the matter?

TILLY   Oh ... it reminds me of my sadness.

FLO   Oh, sorry, I didn't mean to ...

(FLO *reaches to take the cardigan but* TILLY *holds
it close.*)

TILLY	Can I keep it, please, Flo?
FLO	(*gently*) No, give it back. It's not healthy.
TILLY	Please ... ?
FLO	No.
TILLY	Oh, please let me keep it; let me keep it, please.
FLO	(*firmer*) No, Till, give it back to me.
	(TILLY *hands the cardigan back, reluctantly.*)
TILLY	I hope she loves it. I hope she loves her baby.
FLO	I'm sure she does. It's seven months old, now. Sent me a picture last month. (*She fishes the picture out of her bag and hands it to* TILLY.)
	Lovely little thing, isn't he?
TILLY	Ah, look at that. A little Canadian. Ah.
FLO	Wish I could see him in the flesh.
	(JOK *enters. He goes through his paces, rehearsing his coming shots.*)
TILLY	He's gorgeous. (*Tickling the baby's chin on the photo.*) Goochy-woochy.
FLO	Maybe I'll be able to get over there one day.
TILLY	What does she think about you leaving here, your Lilly?
FLO	Haven't told her. She'd only worry herself. She's a good girl, she still writes to me every fortnight.
	(FLO *takes the photo back and returns it to her bag.* TILLY *sniffs the air.*)
TILLY	What's that funny smell?
JOK	Oh, d'you like it? That's my new perfume.
	(*He crosses to them and offers* TILLY *his wrist to sniff, which she does.*)

TILLY	Very smelly. Nice.
	(FLO *wafts away what she regards as an unpleasant odour.* TILLY *looks around at the film equipment.*)
	This is so exciting, all this filming. Never seen anything like this before.
JOK	Yeah, well, when you've done as much as I have it's just a job. Know what I mean? I don't go along with all that star bit. I'm just a working bloke. (*Taking a photograph and pen from his inside pocket.*) What was it you wanted, an autograph?
TILLY	Nah. Just wanted to watch.
JOK	Have one if you want — no problem.
TILLY	I don't need one, thanks.
	(JOK *looks disappointed. He puts the pen and photo back.*)
JOK	Oh.
TILLY	This is my friend, Flo. (*To* FLO.) My friend — er — ?
	(JOK *magnanimously steps forward and offers his hand to* FLO.)
JOK	The name's Jok.
	(FLO *moves her hands out of harm's way.*)
TILLY	(*beaming*) He's famous.
FLO	(*ignoring him*) Don't look famous to me. I've never seen him before.
TILLY	I'm his fan.
FLO	Leave him alone.
JOK	That's all right, love. No problem. I deal with this kind of thing all the time.
TILLY	How many hits have you had?

JOK	Er ... strictly speaking, I've never charted.
FLO	I beg your pardon?
JOK	Charted.
FLO	Oh.
JOK	I'm hoping this is going to be the lucky one.
TILLY	Oh, I'll keep my fingers crossed for you.
JOK	I appreciate that. If we all wish for the same thing ... who knows?

(LUKE *enters with* ROGER.)

LUKE   (*to* JOK) Okay, Marlon, you're on ...

(JOK *crosses to them. They all turn this way and that as* LUKE *points and explains what he wants.* ROGER *makes notes on a clipboard.*)

So what I suggest is ... the ambulance draws up over there. Long-shot. Zoom in. Then a two-shot as the two guys in white coats open the door. Then cut to Jok's P.O.V., the grounds and all the patients shuffling around. Cut to close-up, look of horror on his face. He decides to make a run for it. He shoots over the lawns.

(*He points in the direction* JOK *will run. They turn that way.*)

Nice high shot. Then a two-shot as Jok sees the beautiful girl, Laura-Lee, Katy Baxter, who should be standing here, listening to this, but, of course, she hasn't got out of bed yet. Cut to Jok's face again as he tries to figure out: is it a lunatic or is it Laura-Lee? Am I seeing things? Etcetera. The men in white coats catch up with him, stick a needle in his arm, he becomes quiescent.

JOK   What?

LUKE   They drug you.

(JOK *smiles happily at the mention of drugs*.)

LUKE (*to* ROGER) Put a straight-jacket on him, frog-march him inside, throw him in a locked ward. Okay?

JOK Just one thing — I've been thinking ...

LUKE (*sniffing the air*) What's that funny smell?

JOK Oh, that's my new perfume. Do you like it? (LUKE *turns up his nose*.) It's a special import. Comes in a beautiful flagon. Anyway, I've been having a think ...

LUKE Oh, you have?

JOK Yeah. And I know you won't mind if I make a little improvement here, to your basic idea.

(ROGER *exits, sensing trouble*.)

LUKE Oh yes?

JOK Yeah. I mean: you've got my character going off to the left, right ... ?

LUKE Yes. So?

JOK Well, think about this: the thing you've got to remember about my character is: he's actually handling a lot of pressure. In the sense that he ain't handling it, right? I mean, he's had a breakdown, right? So I think it would be a lot subtler if he weren't to go off to the left, he were to go off to the right. You know, my way you're making a statement: he may not be right *now* but he's *going right*. (LUKE, *dumbstruck, doesn't respond*.) I think that would improve things a lot. What do *you* think?

LUKE (*shaking his head, amazed, beyond anger*) You really are something else.

JOK (*taking it as a compliment*) Yeah, sure ... So, what d'you reckon?

LUKE (*quiet, furious*) I don't value your artistic input.

JOK	(*amazed*) I hope I'm not dealing with what I call "professional jealousy" here, Luke. I thought that was a very good idea, myself. So did my mother.
LUKE	I beg your pardon?
JOK	I discussed my thoughts last night with my mother and she thought it was a great idea, too.
LUKE	Oh well, why didn't you say so before? As long as your *mother* liked it, we're home and dry, aren't we?
JOK	She was a go-go dancer! She knows about these things.
LUKE	The best thing you can do is just ... get into your make-up.
JOK	I *do* know what I'm talking about, Luke. I've done amateur acting in my time.
LUKE	Yes, it shows.
JOK	There we are, you see — you've admitted it.
LUKE	Go and get ready — before I flip?
JOK	I've also done a fair bit of mime, as it happens. That was another important stage in my development. So you think it over.

(*He walks off, proud, head held high.* ROGER *enters.*)

ROGER	(*to* LUKE, *amazed*) Blimey — I've just met a man who thinks he's a dog.
LUKE	What's so funny about that? He thinks he's a singer. Important stage in his development? He's the least developed person I've ever met! Katy Baxter, where is she? Let me talk to her.
ROGER	She's still not here yet, Guv.

LUKE	(*looking at his watch*) Oh, God give me patience. Go and get him out of make-up as soon as you can.
	(ROGER *exits.* LUKE *is just about to leave when* TERRY *enters and approaches him.*)
TERRY	Excuse me, I'm the Health Service Commissioner. I'm here on a secret mission.
LUKE	You're a patient.
TERRY	Yes, being admitted was part of the cover. It's all very hush-hush. Her Majesty's Government are very concerned about the state of the paint in my room and demand that it's re-painted immediately!
TILLY	(*to* TERRY) Leave the man alone, he wants to be private.
	(TERRY *walks away from* LUKE.)
TERRY	Stand at ease! Please. On your knees. And eat your peas. (*Beat.*) Or you'll get fleas. (*Beat.*) They'll make you sneeze. (*Beat.*) School fees. Two teas. That's a wheeze.
	(*He exits.* FLO *marches up to* LUKE.)
FLO	Do I look mad to you?
LUKE	Not at all. No way.
FLO	I'm not. There's nothing wrong with me.
LUKE	I'm sure there isn't.
FLO	The only thing wrong with me is: I've been in this bloody place too long.
LUKE	Sure. I don't believe in mental illness. It's a myth, in my book. I mean we're all mad in one way or another, aren't we? You know, sometimes I think I'm a bit of a schizophrenic, myself. Well, half of me does. Wasn't it Freud who said: "Show me a man who's one hundred-per-cent sane and I'll show you a madman"?

TILLY   Did he?

LUKE   Well, I'll buy that. I mean, I'm a complete
           whacko sometimes. You know, when I'm
           working, if I think the performers need to be
           relaxed, I'll maybe crawl about the floor,
           screaming, making silly faces.

TILLY   Really?

LUKE   Sure, I'll go one hundred-per-cent apeshit if
           it encourages them to relax and put
           themselves on the line. Okay, you might look
           at me and think *I'm* a bit of a lunatic, and,
           sure, I'll admit it. Okay, no hang-ups.
           Because *I* can get away with it. I'm making
           money. You can be as mad as the Taj Mahal
           if it's adding up in the bank. But if I stopped
           making money they'd have me in here
           pronto, locked up with the rest of
           you ... people. I made a video with
           Springsteen, you know?

TILLY   Oh, yeah. Dusty Springsteen.

           (*Beat.*)

LUKE   Yeah ... Anyway, we had thirty naked vicars.
           On trampolines. And it worked. So I'm a
           hero. You've got to be able to *sell* your
           madness. The skid is to make it work for you.
           (*To* FLO.) As it is, you obviously just couldn't
           sell your particular brand of insanity, I'll take
           a bet on it. What was it they hauled you in
           for?

FLO   I used to stand in the parlour window with
           no clothes on. Next to the aspidistra.

           (*Beat.*)

LUKE   Right. That's not something you can market
           very easily.

FLO   Twenty years they've kept me locked up in
           here.

LUKE   What's the point? You've paid the price.
They should have torn these places down
years ago. They're monstrous aberrations.
You ought to be back out there.

FLO   (*suddenly fearful*) No. I can't go out there.

LUKE   Why not?

FLO   No. People know what I'm thinking. They
can read my thoughts. Through the
television set. That's why I have to walk in
straight lines. They're out to get me. I'm safe
in here. See, if you look at me from the side,
you can see I'm Elizabeth Taylor.

LUKE   Oh dear.

FLO   I've got Doris Day's voice. I stole her voice
pattern.

LUKE   Oh. Well, in principle, I still think it's right to
put you back out there, where you belong.
There's no justification for keeping people
incarcerated in a place like this.

(TERRY *enters, highly agitated.*)

TERRY   (*to* LUKE) I'm arresting you! I'm having the
police lock you up!

LUKE   Oh, really. What for?

TERRY   Murder!

LUKE   (*nervously*) Oh. Oh, really? Who have I killed?

TERRY   Me!

(TERRY *spits at* LUKE, *venomously. He realises*
TERRY'S *serious.*)

Keeping me in this fucking place! I'm as
good as dead being here. And you're the
man who murdered me! You gave me
poison. And now I'm going to kill you!
(TERRY *takes out a large kitchen knife from inside
his jacket.* LUKE *jumps back.*)

LUKE   Oh good Jesus!

TILLY   (*concerned, stepping in between them*) Terry!
            Stop it! It wasn't him. He's not a nurse!

TERRY   This is the man who killed my spirit.

TILLY   (*firmly*) Give me that knife before you do
            someone an injury. Give it to Tilly. You'll be
            sorry if you don't.

            (TERRY *looks at her, breathing heavily,
            considering it. He throws the knife to the floor.*
            TILLY *picks it up.* TERRY *sits on the bench.*)

LUKE   I er ... Thank you. I er ... (*He exits.*)

TILLY   Oh, he's lovely, isn't he? A real gentleman. I
            love his manner.

FLO   You've gone off the other fella already, have
            you?

GEORGIE   (*rushing in*) My God, you really are playing
            games today, aren't you, Terry? Come on,
            where is it? (*He approaches* TERRY, *holding out
            his hand.*)

TERRY   I don't know what you're talking about.

GEORGIE   You were seen going into the kitchens. Now
            come on, hand over whatever you took.

TILLY   (*showing* GEORGIE *the knife*) Is this what you're
            looking for, Georgie?

GEORGIE   Oh Jesus. Is that what he's been charging
            around with? (GEORGIE *takes the knife. He goes
            to* TERRY.) You're a naughty boy, Terry. You
            pull another stunt like that and we'll have to
            restrict your movements. In a way you won't
            find pleasant.

TILLY   He wants to go home.

GEORGIE   Yes, well his wife doesn't want him home
            until he's calmed down. And who can blame
            her? (*He starts to exit.*) Thank you, Tilly.

TILLY	(*calling*) Georgie! (GEORGIE *stops, turns.*) I think I'd like to be in the film.
GEORGIE	Don't you think that might be a little unrealistic?
TILLY	No. I could do it. I've always had good expressions. Will you ask them if I can be?
GEORGIE	Certainly not. You're quite capable. Ask yourself.
TILLY	Do you think I should?
GEORGIE	It's up to you.
TILLY	Yeah . . . I think I will.
	(*He goes. She calls again. He stops.*)
	What do you think I should say, Georgie?
GEORGIE	What do *you* think you should say?
TILLY	*I* don't know — that's why I'm asking *you*. I want to ask in the right way.
GEORGIE	Ask if you can make an audition.
TILLY	Yeah, that's the word. Audition. Yeh . . . I will. Thanks, Georgie.
FLO	(*getting up*) Well, can't sit here all day. Got to keep walking. (*She walks over to* TILLY.) You coming?
TILLY	(*irritated, preoccupied*) No.
	(TILLY *goes and* FLO *walks off, wearily, in the opposite direction.* JOK *enters, having emerged from the make-up van with a simulated growth, staring at himself in a hand mirror.*)
JOK	Do you ever have a growth?
TERRY	(*surprised*) I beg your pardon?
JOK	Do you ever get the opportunity to have a growth in your line of business?
TERRY	Business? I'm not in business.

JOK   No — stubble. It's very much a fashion thing at the moment.

(JOK *crosses to* TERRY *on the bench.* TERRY *moves away from him, suspicious.*) I usually go around with a two-day growth, myself. I find a three-day looks a bit heavy.

(TERRY *looks at him as though he's mad.*)

I find the women like it, to be honest. Of course, you do get the kind of woman who goes for a four-day. But I really don't like heavy women.

(TERRY *moves further along the bench.*)

Yeah, I see it very much as a virility thing, a growth. You know, part of my image. My beard's quite tough, actually. Quite dark. Very sensual. Mind you, I'm not saying I don't enjoy a good shave, I do. Don't get me wrong. I enjoy a wet-shave more, though. Dry-shaving's not my cup of tea, in all honesty.

(TERRY *moves further still.* JOK *gets up.*)

Yeah, this is it. I've also been working out very hard in a gym this last year or so. Really toning up those muscles. Getting to grips with my body. Really taking it in hand.

(*He begins to run his hands over his body, admiringly.* TERRY *looks disturbed*).

I'm really very pleased with this new outline.

(*He runs his hand over his groin.*)

It's much better ... better ... there's a word for it. Uh ...

(JOK *turns away from* TERRY, *thinking hard. Beat.* TERRY *shakes his head and exits.* JOK *turns back to* TERRY.)

Yeah, much better "defined".

(*He realises that* TERRY *has fled.*)

Oh. (*Calling after* TERRY.) Much better "defined". Nice bloke. Interesting.

(DICK *enters, flustered.*)

DICK   Ah, Dennis, just the man I've been looking for.

JOK   (*irritated*) Don't call me Dennis, you know how it enrages me! The name's Jok. Okay?

DICK   What have you been saying to my director?

JOK   I just made a few suggestions, that's all, how he could improve the video.

DICK   Listen, don't interfere with the artistic process. Leave it up to his *genius*. What we need here is brilliant image-creation. Because, let's face it, son, with you we're trying to create Wonder Whip out of clipped toenails.

JOK   Oh, thanks a bunch. I'm entitled to have my say. I am an *artiste*, too, you know.

DICK   Just button it.

JOK   I'm free to talk. It's my mouth. (*He walks off.*)

DICK   (*under his breath*) You long streak of piss. You blow this and I'll remove your balls. One by one. With a monkey wrench.

(TILLY *enters and taps* DICK *on the shoulder*.)

TILLY   Excuse me, are you the foreman?

DICK   (*amazed, irritated*) No, I'm not the ruddy foreman. Why? Who are you?

TILLY   Tilly. I'd like to make an audition for a part in your film, please.

DICK   (*looking at her, amused*) Have you had much training, love?

TILLY   Oh yeah, I've seen lots of films. All the
                 classics.

DICK   Reckon you could be a pin-up, then, do you?
                 (*He moves to his little table and opens his
                 briefcase.*)

TILLY   No. More a sort of character.

DICK   Yeah, well at least you've got some brains left.

TILLY   Can I make an audition, please?

DICK   Who do you think would want to look at you
                 on the screen?

TILLY   My friends. They'd love it. And I've always
                 had good expressions.

DICK   (*gently*) Hop it. Go on. Buzz off.

                 (*Pause.* TILLY *is offended. She walks away, stops,
                 turns.*)

TILLY   I gave you the opportunity to discover me.
                 One day you'll regret this.

                 (FLO *enters.*)

DICK   That's something I'll just have to learn to live
                 with, then, isn't it?

TILLY   (*bitter; almost angry*) You mark my words.

DICK   (*tired of it now*) Bugger off. Go and do some
                 basket-weaving!

                 (*That is a red rag to a bull.* TILLY *begins to fume
                 quietly. She decides to stand her ground.*)

TILLY   Can I have a reason why I can't audition for
                 your film?

DICK   I don't have to give you a ruddy reason.

TILLY   (*firm*) I realise that. I were just wondering if
                 you'd be courteous enough to.

                 (DICK *looks at* TILLY *and* FLO.)

DICK   Right. Let me teach you a couple of things.

            (*He bends close, talks to them as though they were
            mentally-defective.*)

            (*pointing*) Over there is a lot of very
            expensive equipment. Worth more, probably,
            than all you little patients, put together,
            could earn in a lifetime. There are also a lot
            of highly-paid, very skilful people with a lot
            of expertise. That means they're experts.

            (TILLY *stares at him icily, unassuaged.*)

            Now the last thing they want is to have a
            bunch of ... you people, scrambling around,
            making funny noises like: "Ooh", "aah",
            "that's how it's done"; tripping over the
            equipment and making a bloody nuisance of
            yourselves. You get me? Making movies is a
            serious business.

TILLY   We wouldn't be any trouble.

DICK   No.

TILLY   *You* watch *us*, all the time.

DICK   That's different.

TILLY   Why is it?

DICK   I've got better things to do than stand
            arguing the toss with you.

TILLY   (*her anger rising*) *Why* is it different?

FLO   (*trying to diffuse the tension*) That's it, then,
            Tilly, he's given it the cold shoulder.

DICK   You're a bright girl. You've got the message.

TILLY   You bad-mannered twerp!

DICK   Now look, you — on your bike!

TILLY   (*angry*) You keep a civil tongue in your face
            when you talk to me. I've had dinner with
            Royalty. I've eaten off silver-plate in my time.
            Don't you treat me like a toe-rag.

FLO   Come on, Till, you'll only upset yourself.

TILLY   You bastard, you!

FLO   She's highly-strung.

DICK   Better take her away and give her a cold shower, then. (*He exits.*)

TILLY   (*shouting after him*) I'll have you, mister! Coming here giving us stick. I could have you locked in the Bloody Tower. I could have you hung, drawn and quartered. (*She turns back to* FLO.) Prat!

             (*They walk off together.*)

             (*Quick fade.*)

Scene Three

The gardens, two hours later.

The film-makers' paraphernalia has been cleared to one side and the garden has become the set, ready for shooting.

Three or four mannequins are scattered around the garden.

JOK *is sitting on the floor, repeating a buddhist chant.* TILLY *and* FLO *watch him with attentive incomprehension.*

LUKE *enters, followed by* ROGER.

LUKE   Okay, Jok, mate. I just want you to walk up and down looking a bit mad.

             (JOK *walks up and down, stiff and straight, looking completely normal apart from a raised eyebrow and a mad, staring eye.*)

             Yeah, that's ... good, Jok. Very good. Some interesting things happening there. It's just that the guy has gone *completely* loopy and we are in long-shot, so we need to see the man's insanity a bit more.

JOK   Oh. Right. No problem.

               (JOK *walks up and down again but this time he*
               goes to the other extreme — dreadful 'mad' acting.
               Plus a limp.)

LUKE   Yes, well, that was certainly less subtle, Jok.
               Lose half of that, elbow the limp and I think
               we're home and dry.

JOK   (*surprised, disappointed*) Elbow the limp? Limps
               have always been a bit of a speciality of mine.

LUKE   Some other time? Go and get ready.

               (LUKE *turns away from* JOK. JOK *exits.*)

JOK   (*as he goes, angry*) Elbow the limp!

LUKE   (*to* ROGER) Right, let's push on. Katy Baxter,
               where is she?

ROGER   We're still trying to locate her, Guv'nor.

LUKE   (*angry*) Oh, that's going to look great on film
               — a big empty patch where our leading lady
               should be. What are we going to do, scratch
               in the words: "Sorry, couldn't find her"?

ROGER   What do you suggest, Guv?

LUKE   You'd better go and ask the "Producer".
               (ROGER *exits.* LUKE *turns to* TILLY *and* FLO.)
               That reptilian Churchill? He bears as much
               relation to a real producer as my arse to a
               pink orchid.

               (LUKE *exits.* GEORGIE *enters.*)

GEORGIE   Tilly, the staff want to see you at twelve
               o'clock.

TILLY   Okay, Georgie.

GEORGIE   Be here ten minutes before and I'll take you
               in.

TILLY   Oh, right. Thanks, Georgie. (GEORGIE *walks*
               off. He stops momentarily, looks at the

mannequins, shakes his head and exits.) I hate
going before that lot. I get all nervous and
my mouth goes dry. (*She smoothes her clothes.*)
How do I look?

FLO   Very nice. What you going to say when you
              get in there?

TILLY   (*preparing herself*) I'll walk in, I'll sit down, I'll
              pause, swallow, and then I'll say: (*she takes a
              deep breath and blurts it out, angrily*) "You
              bastards, you sent me away to the seaside,
              you don't know what it's like sitting on the
              prom eating fish-paste sandwiches, I haven't
              even got a rain-hat and I miss my friends,
              you bastards!"

              (*Pause.* FLO *considers it. She looks doubtful.*)

FLO   That's nice.

TILLY   Yeah, it's nice, it's direct, it's to the point, but
              it makes me sound ridiculous. I've got to put
              it in a way they understand. I've got to be
              logical, concise, pertinent. As opposed to
              impertinent, which'll get me nowhere. You've
              gotta remember that these are the kind of
              people think jogging is the solution to
              everything. You see my point?

FLO   (*after considering it*) No.

TILLY   I mean: I can't barge in and attack them. I've
              got to get them on my side.

FLO   They'll think you're mad, wanting to come
              and live back here. You do realise that?

TILLY   Well, I think *they're* mad for putting us back
              out *there*.

FLO   I'm afraid I'd have to agree with *them* more
              than with *you*.

TILLY   Oh, would you now?

FLO	Oh yes. It must be lovely to be back in the community again. To meet new people. Make new friends. To roam around free, as the spirit takes you. Maybe pop in to the Odeon now and again or a jumble sale and that kind of thing. You won't catch me coming back here. No fear.
TILLY	Oh, you'd know, I suppose, Flo. You're the expert. Half an hour ago, you were saying you didn't want to leave.
FLO	Well, this is the thing. Half of me wants to go — and half of me doesn't. I feel in two minds about it, really.
TILLY	What do you think's waiting for you out there? A welcoming party and a brass band with banners saying: "good old Flo, glad to have you back."
FLO	No, but . . .
TILLY	Because if that's what you're expecting, you'd better think again.
FLO	Yes, but you can choose what time you go to bed.
TILLY	Yeah, but the difference is . . . Out there, Flo, you don't want to go to bed.
FLO	(*quickly, disbelieving, almost telling* TILLY *off*) Everyone wants to go to bed. That's silly, to say you don't want to go to bed.
TILLY	But you don't want to go to bed in a room full of strangers who fart in their sleep.
FLO	Ooh, dreadful. Terrible habit.
TILLY	Yeh, you don't mind if it's a friend, but . . .
FLO	Must be lovely, the sea air, though. Taking a stroll along the prom. Fishing boats bobbing up and down on the sea and that kind of

thing. People paint pictures of seaside views and stick them on their living room walls. That's how popular they are.

TILLY   Yeah but they don't paint pictures of the pissing rain, do they?

FLO   Well, no, but who'd want a picture of the pissing rain? People tend to paint what they can sell, don't they?

TILLY   I don't think we're getting very far, are we, Flo?

FLO   No. I'll go in for cream teas and things like that. Clotted cream. Scones. Strawberry jam. Marvellous.

TILLY   Where's the money coming from?

FLO   Well, it'd be provided . . .

TILLY   Who by?

FLO   Well, I don't know. There must be some charity or other out there giving money for clotted cream teas for ex-mental patients.

TILLY   And I suppose you think you'll have a nice little room of your own, in a nice little hotel, with a kettle in the corner and tea-bags and a packet of Rich Tea . . .

FLO   Naturally.

TILLY   And the occasional holiday. And enough money to live on and decent clothes to wear and lots of friends and . . . and . . . all that sort of stuff.

FLO   Well, I hope that that's the minimum we can expect. Otherwise there's no point in us leaving, is there?

TILLY   Oh, Flo. If things were so nice, why d'you think I ended up sleeping rough on the beach with all the other ex-patients? Why do you think I decided to come back here?

FLO   Well, this is the thing. I *thought* it was a
               strange thing to do.

               (ROGER *enters, finds Jok's mark, looks off to check
               that it's okay and gives the thumbs up. His walkie
               talkie crackles into life.*)

ROGER   (*talking into it*) Hello, Roger here, over. (*He
               listens.*) Roger, go ahead, over. (*Listens.*) Oh
               my God, over. (*Listens.*) Oh dear God, he's
               going to have a heart attack. Over. (*Listens.*)
               No, he's with the crew. We're just about to do
               a take. I'll tell him. Over and out. (*He looks at
               TILLY and FLO.*) He's gonna die on the spot.
               Either that or he's gonna murder somebody.

TILLY   Is everything okay?

ROGER   Okay, she says. Oh, wonderful. Marvellous.
               Great! (*He exits.*)

TILLY   He seems a bit flustered.

FLO   He's not the only one, Till. These things
               you're telling me . . . aren't there any decent
               places to live out there?

TILLY   The nice houses won't take discharged
               patients in. They say we scare off the
               commercial travellers.

FLO   Oh, charming.

TILLY   We're not welcome anywhere. That's why you
               have to sit on the prom all day, whiling away
               your life. Trying to steer clear of the trawlers.

FLO   The what? What's a trawler?

TILLY   The dirty-raincoat brigade. They trawl up
               and down the seafront offering women a
               place to stay or a meal if you'll . . . you
               know . . . go with them.

FLO   Go with them where?

TILLY	No. You know, *go* with them.
	(TILLY *nods.* FLO *doesn't get it.* TILLY *nods again.*)
FLO	Go *where* with them?
TILLY	*Go* with them. You know, in the biblical sense. Do funny things with them. To their rude bits. Behind the bushes. In the lavatories.
	(*Slowly,* FLO *gets it.*)
FLO	That's disgusting.
TILLY	I know it is. They think ex-patients are easy meat. Mind you, I know some women who've had to give in to them. Just to get a bit of a feed.
FLO	And these are *fishermen*, are they?
TILLY	No, trawlers is just what we call them. You know, a *joke* name.
FLO	But people like that aren't *funny*.
TILLY	(*putting her arms around* FLO'S *shoulders*) I know, Flo. I know. Your problem is you've been in here too long, my pet. You've lost touch with the outside world.
FLO	Thank God I have.
	(ROGER *enters, holding* JOK'S *arm. He places him on his mark.* JOK *wears a straight-jacket. He takes off his shades and hands them to* ROGER.)
ROGER	That's your mark, mate, okay?
JOK	Okey-dokey. (*He sits amongst the mannequins.*)
ROGER	(*into his walkie-talkie*) Right, Jok's in first position. Are the ladies all right? (*He listens. Then to* TILLY *and* FLO.) Stay where you are please, ladies, and don't move. We're just about to shoot. I'll give you a signal, Jok.

(*Silence.* TILLY *freezes.* ROGER *and* JOK *both wait, expectantly.* TILLY *and* FLO *look on with great interest. A warning bell rings to signify the start of filming.*)

TILLY   I love all this film stuff . . .

ROGER   Quiet please, ladies!

(TILLY *goes back to her 'frozen' position. Silence. Tension. The music starts, then we hear* LUKE'S *distant voice shouting through a megaphone.*)

LUKE   (*off*) Okay, nice and still now. And . . . action.

ROGER   Action, please, Jok!

(JOK *moves up and down doing 'mad' acting, as the music plays.* TILLY *and* FLO *look at each other. At the climax of the 'take',* JOK, *acting breathless and insane, rushes towards the gate, sees an imaginary 'Laura-Lee' and freezes.*)

LUKE   (*off*) And . . . cut!

ROGER   Okay, cut it! Hold still, please!

(JOK *relaxes. The music stops, and the 'all clear' bell sounds.*)

JOK   That was fine for me.

ROGER   Just a mo', we might be going again. Nice work, Jok.

JOK   Thanks.

ROGER   No, they're gonna print that. New set-up. Relax.

JOK   (*as he exits*) I still think it would have been better with a limp. But . . . what can you do?

LUKE   (*entering from the opposite direction*) Right, let's get a bit of flow on this . . .

FLO   (*standing, expectantly*) Yes?

(*They ignore her. She sits, disappointed.*)

LUKE   Okay, so the next set-up is inside the ward.
            Let's get that in before lunch, then Laura-
            Lee ...

ROGER   Guv'nor ...

LUKE   Yes?

ROGER   I thought it would be better if you got that
            shot in the can before I gave you the news,
            Guv'nor.

LUKE   What news?

ROGER   (*backing off a little*) We've lost our leading
            lady, Laura-Lee, Guv. Katy Baxter's not on
            her way at all. She's had a bit of a disaster
            with a chip-pan. She's in Intensive Care.

LUKE   Oh my God. Don't. She can't be.

ROGER   She was frying chips in her kitchen last night,
            set fire to herself. Her face has gone,
            apparently.

LUKE   Oh my good Jesus. (*He lets out a huge scream.*)

ROGER   I know how you feel, Guv.

FLO   (*to* TILLY) He's got a screw loose.

ROGER .   She's still alive, if that's any consolation.

DICK   (*entering, flustered*) You've heard our leading
            lady's had her chips, then?

LUKE   This is a nightmare.

            (LUKE *paces up and down.* TERRY *enters. He
            paces, too, copying them.*)

DICK   It's gonna take half a bloody day to find a
            replacement. Now I'm really up shit creek.
            Silly cow. I'd like to go over to that bloody
            hospital and pull the plug on her.

ROGER   At least she'll be fine for a remake of *The
            Invisible Man*, all them bandages.

DICK   So what do we do?

LUKE	I don't know. Send her flowers or something?
DICK	I'm not talking about her. I'm talking about *us*. I'd better get on the blower, get a replacement. God Almighty ... (*He exits with* TERRY *following.*)
LUKE	Filming in a real loony bin — you must be mad, they said. It's too risky, they said. Do it in a studio, they said. No way, I said. It'll be fine, I said. It'll look great. I *must* be bloody mad.
	(LUKE *sits and holds his head in his hands. Then he looks up, at* TILLY. *She notices his gaze.*)
TILLY	You're not a trawler, are you?
LUKE	Yes — not as mad as it seems ...
TILLY	Mad? I'm not mad anything, mate. I just get ill now and again.
LUKE	(*to* ROGER) Look at those cheeks. And those eyes.
FLO	People like you can be prosecuted, I warn you. You touch her and I'll make a citizen's arrest.
LUKE	She's our replacement. (*To* TILLY.) You're my Laura-Lee. (*To* ROGER.) Get hold of Dick.
FLO	Don't you mention dick to her, she's convent-educated.
ROGER	(*from the side of his mouth*) I have to point out to you, Guv'nor, that she's away-with-the-mixer. One of the inmates.
FLO	You just be very careful, the pair of you. I knew a man who did Karate.
LUKE	(*to* ROGER) Go and get him.
FLO	(*thinking he means her*) I will!
	(*She walks off in the opposite direction, then suddenly stops, realising she doesn't know him any more.* ROGER *exits.*)

LUKE	(*to* TILLY) Have you ever been in a film?
TILLY	Not a video-nasty, is it?
LUKE	I'd like you to be my Laura-Lee.
TILLY	(*excited*) What would I have to do?
LUKE	Well, in that caravan over there is the star of our little film.
TILLY	Yes, I know. (*Playing it down.*) Tall, good-looking one. I do believe I've seen him around, yes.
LUKE	Well, this place is a lunatic asylum ...
TILLY	Yes, I know that.
LUKE	And his girlfriend, Laura-Lee, has left him, you see. So he has a breakdown. And he's carted off and keeps seeing her everywhere and he thinks you're really Laura-Lee, but, in fact, you're just an inmate of the asylum.
TILLY	I am, that's right. Well, was. Well, will be.
LUKE	It'd be just a matter of him ... embracing you and ... kissing you and ... this kind of thing.
	(TILLY *looks at* FLO.)
TILLY	(*hiding her delight*) Oh yes?
FLO	(*perturbed*) What kind of film is this?
LUKE	You've no objections?
TILLY	No. Not really. If it's for the good of the film, I could put up with it.
LUKE	Good. Excellent. Right, come on, I'll take you to wardrobe.
	(LUKE *puts his arm around her and they move off.* TILLY *suddenly stops.*)
TILLY	Oh, I can't now.

LUKE	Don't be worried about holes in your knickers. We've seen it all before.
TILLY	No, it's not that. I've got to go before the staff.
LUKE	How long will this take?
TILLY	Oh, only half-an-hour, at the most. Wait for me, please.
LUKE	Okay, fine. It'll take us that long to set up. Very good. Excellent. (*He exits, pleased.*)
TILLY	(*twirling around*) I'm gonna be featured.
FLO	Oh, here we go again.
TILLY	I'm gonna be prominent. With hunky-chunky.
FLO	Now you keep your feet on the ground.
TILLY	I always knew I had star quality. This is the break I've been looking for.
FLO	Oh dear, it's gone to her head already. You're gonna be unbearable.
TILLY	I don't know who to model myself on for the best results.
FLO	The shape of you, I should think the leaning tower of Pisa.
TILLY	You can't knock me. I'm above all that now. I'm going to be rich. I'm going to be famous.
FLO	Now don't go off into another world, you know what you're like.
TILLY	I shall take you everywhere I go. You can be my lady-in-waiting. You'll be salaried.
FLO	I've been salaried before. I was once heavily involved with the lower ranks of the Civil Service.

TILLY   We'll travel the world. In comfort and style.
                 The way it used to be in the old days. We'll
                 have leather suitcases with straps. We'll have
                 them initialled.

FLO   Monogrammed.

TILLY   We'll have that, too. We'll stroll up the
                 gangplank. Travel first-class. Port out,
                 starboard home. I've always wanted to be
                 posh. We'll stay in all the best hotels. Meet
                 interesting people. Princes and the like. I'll
                 offer my hand.

FLO   Give it a good scrub first.

TILLY   It'll be kissed in the moonlight by self-made
                 millionaires. I'll be seduced under palm-trees
                 by men who are big in steel.

FLO   That'll make a change from the cricket
                 pavilion.

TILLY   Oh, we'll have a wonderful time, Flo. We'll be
                 invited for barbecues on board the royal
                 yacht, Britannia. I'll wear sable and mink,
                 with a hint of ermine.

FLO   With a hint of vermin? What do you want to
                 wear vermin for?

TILLY   Ermine. Not vermin.

FLO   Oh.

TILLY   I'll have black and white stills taken for the
                 fans to cherish. You can sign them on my
                 behalf.

FLO   You'd have to give me a Biro.

TILLY   Oh, of course. I'll leave my footprints in the
                 pavement outside that Chinese take-away in
                 Hollywood, along with all the other greats of
                 the silver screen. Garbo and Valentino,
                 Cagney and Lacey, Chips Rafferty and me —
                 Tilly Jane Armitage. Oh, there are so many

wonderful things to do out there. So many
beautiful places to see, people to meet. I
want to meet them all, see everything before
I die.

(*Suddenly* FLO *bursts into tears.* TILLY *crosses to
her.*)

Hey, hey, what's the matter?

FLO   I'm ... I'm gonna die without seeing *any* of
those things.

TILLY   Aw, you're a long way off dying, what's the
matter with you?

FLO   I'll end my days in an old seaside hotel with
dry skin and laddered stockings in a house
that smells of cabbages and piss. Oh, Tilly,
sometimes I wish I was dead.

TILLY   (*comforting her*) Come on, you're not half
dead, yet.

FLO   What's gonna happen to me when they send
me away to the seaside? I don't know
anybody. I don't even like the bloody sea.
Can't even swim. Even if I could swim,
haven't got a cozzie. What am I gonna do —
skinny-dip? Eh? With a figure like mine? No
shark'd come near me, I can tell you. They
see this shape swimming towards them,
they'd bugger off, sharpish. They know
which side their bread's buttered.

(DICK *marches on, looking extremely flustered. He
is followed by* LUKE *and* ROGER. LUKE *goes to*
TILLY.)

LUKE   You said pull something out of the hat for
you. Well, here she is!

DICK   Are you out of your mind?

LUKE   It's inspired.

DICK   It's lunacy.

LUKE	Have you any better ideas?
DICK	Don't be so bloody ridiculous. You can't use her — she's got nothing in the till.
LUKE	If we wait for a replacement, we'll lose half a day.
DICK	Look, we've got enough problems as it is without you doing a bloody Fellini.
LUKE	She's perfect. She's authentic.
DICK	She's only pulling on one oar.
LUKE	We've got no option. Don't worry, I can handle it. I've shot a pop video starring twelve thousand frogs.
DICK	It'll backfire, like a fart from an elephant's arsehole.
LUKE	Twelve thousand frogs. That's a lot of frogs.
DICK	(*growing more and more uncontrolled*) Yeah, well they obviously had all their marbles. This one ain't. She might throw a wobbler. Bite the bleeding ankles of the chippie or something. I don't know, you can never tell with these characters. They're fine one minute and the next they've got the screaming ab-dabs, frothing at the mouth and all manner of madness.
ROGER	(*out of the side of his mouth, to* DICK) He may have a point, Guv. All she has to do is stand there and look gormless. (*They all turn to face her.*) Let's face it, she's half-way there already.
TILLY	(*angrily walking over to them*) I don't only do gormless, you know. I can do any kind of expression you want. Let me prove my skills to you, that's all I ask.
LUKE	What did I tell you — she's a natural.

DICK   No way. Never. I won't allow it. Not in a
                million, bloody years. Clear enough?

                (DICK *storms off.* LUKE *turns to* TILLY.)

LUKE   Sorry. It was just an idea. (*To* ROGER.) Okay,
                let's go on. (*He makes to leave.* TILLY *runs in
                front of him and stops him.*)

TILLY   No. I'm not just an idea. I'm a person. You
                can't just dismiss me like that. My mind's
                made up now. I want my part.

LUKE   I'm sorry. He's given it the cold shoulder. (*To*
                ROGER.) Let's do the running track.

TILLY   No. You can't just ... pick me up and throw
                me down. I've got feelings. You promised me
                a job.

LUKE   I'm sorry. Okay?

TILLY   That's no good to me. I need that job. I want
                to be normal. I want to get back on my feet.
                You promised.

LUKE   It's not possible.

TILLY   But you ... built me up. Now you've gotta
                do something with me.

LUKE   It was just an idea, okay? That didn't go
                anywhere.

TILLY   No, you bastard!

                (*He walks away. She runs at him. She jumps on
                his back and begins to hit him.*)

LUKE   What the hell? Get off!

TILLY   You bastard. You rotten, stinking bastard!

ROGER   Hey, hey, you can't jump on the Guv'nor.

LUKE   Get her off me.

TILLY   I hate you, you rotten, stinking swine.

                (ROGER *pulls her off. He drops her to the floor.*)

LUKE   Jesus. This is what happens when you try to
            help these people. (ROGER *and* LUKE *exit.*)

TILLY   You're just like everyone else. I thought you
            were different. I thought you wanted to help
            me. I thought you *cared* about me.

            (*The lights fade.*)

            END OF ACT ONE

ACT TWO

Scene One

A couple of hours later. A large recreation hall, with a small stage at the rear. An exercise horse, mannequins and the paraphernalia of film-making spread around the hall.

On stage is a tea urn. Sitting next to the urn, unnoticed by DICK *and* LUKE, *is* TILLY, *lost in thought.* LUKE *sits on a chair, some way off from* TILLY, *reading a newspaper.* JOK *sits close to* TILLY, *buried in an ostentatiously large book.* DICK *is sitting, his briefcase open by his side, a pile of bills and papers on his lap. His mood is low, downbeat.*

The door opens and ROGER *enters with two large cans of petrol.*

DICK   What the bloody hell have you brought
                petrol indoors for? You trying to kill us all?

ROGER   I brought them in for safety's sake, Guv'nor.
                One of the . . . (*He looks at* TILLY.) . . . that
                lot . . . was trying to nick the bloody stuff.

DICK   Oh my God, as if we haven't got enough
                problems. Put something over it, then. Cover
                the bloody things up. (*Looking at his wad of
                bills.*) Look at this — bills, bills, bills. Threats
                of prosecution from all and sundry. To think
                people once had high hopes for the
                nationalised industries, Roger.

ROGER   That a fact, Guv?

DICK   Thought they were gonna liberate the
                working man. And what's become of that
                noble dream? Threats of prosecution and
                imprisonment. All instruments of terror.
                What a wicked world it is when you're short
                of greenbacks. Every bloody day some sod
                wants another piece of my flesh. I don't know
                how we're gonna survive, Rog. After this
                we've got nothing. I mean look what they
                give us, the record company — Jok the jerk.

The tartan pillock. He's as tuneful as a wet
fart. I can sing better in the bath.
Underwater. With laryngitis. I begged them,
all the companies, give me a Michael Jackson
or a Prince or Pink Floyd. Let me prove my
"metal" with a Madonna. But no, they give
me the rubbish. All the top artistes go to the
cowboys. The street-cred, smart-arsed, rip-off
merchants. Those buggers have got this
industry sewn up. The Wardour Street
piranhas. We've got to find a higher profile,
Rog.

ROGER   Yeah. We've been too low for too long,
            Guv'nor.

DICK   We've got to find some gimmick that will sort
            us out from all the other Soho whitebait and
            project us into the big tank along with the
            other big fish. I've learned my lesson. It's no
            use being sensitive. Someone sensitive like me
            finds it hard to survive. I've got to become as
            big a bastard as all the others. We're in Shit
            Street, Rog, without a paddle. There's no
            two-ways about it. I hate to say this, but I
            think I might have to lay you off at the end
            of this shoot.

ROGER   You what?

DICK   There's nothing in the pipeline, old son. Not
            even a sausage.

ROGER   What are you talking about?

DICK   I'm sorry, old sport. You know I'd rather
            slash my own throat than let you go but ...

ROGER   Oh, great. Thanks a bunch. (*As he exits in
            disgust.*) Now he tells me!

DICK   Well there's no need to take it personally.
            (*Exiting.*) What's got into him?

TILLY   (*coming forward*) Is it okay if I have a tea,
            please?

LUKE   Of course it is. Look, you can have whatever
            you want, okay? Have a piece of fruit-cake.
            (*Suddenly realising what he's said.*) Oh my God.
            It's good. *Really* good.

TILLY   What you all come here for? To take the piss
            out of the loonies? Prove how funny we all
            are?

LUKE   Not at all.

TILLY   Well what was all that for outside? All that
            screaming and stuff?

LUKE   It's supposed to be like a nightmare.

TILLY   Where you see anyone here walking around
            in a straight-jacket?

LUKE   Well ... that's ... emblematic.

TILLY   Embla-bollocks.

LUKE   Well ... it's ...

TILLY   If that's what you lot out there think life is
            like in here, no wonder we've got bloody
            problems when we go back into the
            community. You ought to be ashamed of
            yourself.

LUKE   I'm sorry. I ...

            (*He doesn't know what to say, so he exits.* JOK
            looks up from his tome.)

JOK   I'd like to share my thoughts about
            something that happened to me yesterday.

TILLY   Oh yeah? (*She crosses to him, sits at his feet.*)

JOK   Yeah. Something strange. (*Closing his book.*)
            Very weird, in fact. I was walking along the
            road, middle of town. I had the shades on,
            'cos I didn't fancy any hassles. You know,
            from the fans. And I was just about to cross
            the road at a main junction. And, as I'm
            standing there, I see, out of the corner of my

eye — not because I was looking, particularly, he just happened to be there — I see a very famous face. Long, blond hair, expensive leather jacket, nice cords. That's a face I know really well, I thought. He's in the music business and obviously doing very well for himself from the state of his togs — and the fact that I recognise him. (TILLY *yawns.*) I didn't want to say anything, 'cos it's such a drag when people molest you on the streets when you're in the public eye, as I'm only too aware. But it was driving me mad, not knowing which band he was in. So I plucked up the courage to put the question to him. "I've been standing here trying to figure out where I know you from," I said, "I know I know you from somewhere." "Yeah, probably," he said, "I work in the Pizza Express." (*Beat.*) I tell you . . .

(JOK *looks at* TILLY *as though the meaning of the story was obvious.* GEORGIE *enters.*)

GEORGIE   Er . . . Dennis your people want a word with you.

JOK   (*getting up*) *Whom?* Well . . . must press on. Get a few more feet in the can. Ciao. Catch you later.

(JOK *exits.* GEORGIE'S *mood is tentative.* TILLY *senses it.*)

TILLY   Yes, Georgie?

GEORGIE   The staff have made their decision.

TILLY   Yes. Very good, Georgie.

GEORGIE   The news *isn't* good, I'm afraid.

TILLY   No, Georgie.

GEORGIE   They say you must leave by the end of the day. You have to go back to the seaside.

(*Beat.* TILLY *is very depressed.*)

Tilly . . . ? You understand?

TILLY   Yes, Georgie. I've got to go back on the
             streets.

GEORGIE   I'm very sorry.

TILLY   That's all right. It's not your fault.

GEORGIE   There's no future here, Tilly. Soon this place
             won't even exist.

TILLY   I know, Georgie.

GEORGIE   (*coming closer to her*) What's the matter?

TILLY   It's all gone wrong, Georgie. It hasn't worked
             out like I wanted it to at all.

GEORGIE   What hasn't?

TILLY   My life. Nothing.

GEORGIE   Aw, come on now.

TILLY   I'm a failure. In everything I've ever tried to
             do. My whole life is a mess. I was a well
             person, once. I was normal, just like everyone
             else. I had a mother that loved me. I had my
             babies. How did I ever get into this mess,
             Georgie? I used to have such dreams of being
             things but look at me now: A tramp. A
             vagrant.

GEORGIE   You're much more than that, Tilly.

TILLY   I can't face going out there again. People are
             so cruel. They taunt you. Call you nasty
             names. Some even called me a whore. I'm a
             God-fearing person. I've never been that way
             inclined. I've had people spit on me. Dirty
             beasts who've spat all over my best coat. So
             you go into a café for a bit of safety and they
             refuse to serve you 'cos they say you put
             people off their food. What an awful thing to
             say. Think I was Quasimodo or the bloody
             Elephant Man. Nobody eating a bit of
             bacon's gonna be put off by the likes of me,
             are they, Georgie?

GEORGIE   Of course not, my angel.

TILLY   Makes me feel awful.

GEORGIE   Oh, darling, what are we going to do? I'd let
            you come and live with me, but the wife'd
            only get jealous.

TILLY   I just don't want to go back to a life without
            hope, Georgie. I'm just a normal human
            being. I can't live without hope.

            (FLO *enters. She is frightened and agitated.*)

FLO   Georgie, I've been bitten by a tropical spider.

GEORGIE   Oh, Flo.

FLO   Someone put it in my handbag. They're
            trying to kill me. (GEORGIE *goes to her.*) They
            know I can see through them, all of them out
            there. I'd rather take an overdose than be
            strangled out there.

GEORGIE   Why would anyone want to kill you?

FLO   I'm dying, Georgie. There's no cure for me.
            Can you give me a blood test? To find out
            what's bitten me? My bed's got killer spiders
            in it. They want me dead. (*He puts his arm
            around her, to comfort her.*) Georgie, put me on
            something to make me happy.

GEORGIE   If that were possible, I would.

FLO   Why can't I have E.C.T.? That will make me
            well. Take away these horrible thoughts from
            my mind. Give it to me, please, Georgie.

GEORGIE   Giving you E.C.T. is not a sign that we care
            about you.

FLO   It'll take my worries away.

GEORGIE   If it did that, my darling, I'd be on it myself.

            (FLO *starts repeating the same peculiar gesture
            over and over again.*)

TILLY	Don't do that, it's not good for you, Flo.
FLO	It's my habit. (GEORGIE *walks* FLO *to the door.*) I don't want to leave here. I don't want to be thrown out. Do something for me, Georgie. Help me, please. Please, Georgie.
GEORGIE	I'll get someone to give you something. You lie down for an hour, you'll feel a lot better.

(GEORGIE *takes* FLO *to the door and calls out:* "*Mrs. Chowdry*". FLO *exits.* GEORGIE *comes back in.*)

TILLY	I feel terrible now. Flo's only in that state because I worried her. I told her how awful things were outside. I thought she was strong enough. I didn't mean to upset her, Georgie. I should have told her I was having the time of my life. I should have said I had a job and a nice place to live and money and ... and people being nice to me and ... (*She's crying.*) It's all my fault. How's Flo gonna cope out there?
GEORGIE	Hey, now come on, you're being silly.
TILLY	What will happen when this place has gone, Georgie? If I haven't got you and my friends, I'm frightened I'll get ill again. And I'll try to kill myself. And this time there'll be no one around to stop me.
GEORGIE	Come on, things aren't as bad as all that.
TILLY	(*cold, hard*) Is there no hope for me, Georgie? Am I going to die? Why do I have to die?

(*Silence.* TILLY *cries.* GEORGIE *tries to remain professionally detached. He can't. He goes to her. He grips her shoulders, almost shaking her.*)

GEORGIE	(*forcefully*) Now listen to me, Tilly. You know I've never lied to you. You're not a fool. I'm not going to give you false comfort. I'm not going to pretend that this isn't a danger. But

	it's not inevitable. You're a fighter. I know you of old. You're a very strong girl when you want to be.

TILLY

Not any more, Georgie. I may as well top myself.

GEORGIE

Now I don't want to hear this silly talk.

TILLY

I'm mentally ill. I need looking after. I can't do it on my own.

(*Pause.*)

GEORGIE

(*quietly, almost apologetic*) I'm afraid the only thing I can offer you is an injection. To help you get through the next few days.

TILLY

(*irritated, angry*) No, Georgie. I don't want the liquid cosh. I've had enough of all that. (*Pause.* GEORGIE *walks away from her a little.*) I'm sorry, Georgie. I don't mean to seem ungrateful, I know you'd help me if you could. I'm sorry. I'll be all right. I'll get by. I always have. You go and see Flo. I'll be fine. Honestly. Thanks.

(GEORGIE *walks slowly towards the door. He stops and turns to* TILLY.)

GEORGIE

You know, I've been wondering for a long time myself: what the hell am *I* going to do when this place is gone? I've got nowhere to go, either. (*He exits.*)

(TILLY *walks around the room, preoccupied, distracted. Then she notices the cans of petrol. She goes to them and takes the cover off them. She looks at the cans for a moment and then walks around the camera. She touches it, gingerly. Then pushes it forward slightly. She stands back and looks at it.* ROGER *enters with the brass dedication plaque and a clip-board.*)

ROGER

Hey you, come on, out of here. This is rented space. We can't have the likes of you in here. This is very expensive equipment. (*He puts the plaque down.*)

TILLY	What do you think I'm going to do, eat it?
ROGER	Don't you try and be clever with me, my girl.
TILLY	(*walking over to him*) I want to see your superiors.
ROGER	You what?
TILLY	The one with the cigar. And the other one.
ROGER	Oh yes? What's your business with them, then?
TILLY	It's very important.
ROGER	You tell me first. They're very busy men.
TILLY	Tell them it's a matter of life and death.

(*Pause.* ROGER, *suspicious, thinks about it.*)

ROGER	I'll see if they're available. And don't go laying your maulers on any of this equipment.

(*As* ROGER *is about to exit,* DICK *enters, carrying a large old-fashioned restraining chair, with leather straps attached to its arms and back. It has a 'lot' number and a 'sold' label stuck on it.*)

ROGER	Er ... this one wants a word with you, Guv'nor. Says it's a matter of life and death.
DICK	(*ignoring her, more interested in his chair*) Oh yeah? Here we are, what do you think of that, then?

(LUKE *enters, he goes to* ROGER *and takes the clip-board from him and begins to read it.*)

ROGER	Very nice. What is it?
DICK	Guess.
ROGER	A commode. You know, one of them chairs you —
DICK	(*cutting him off*) No, you noodle.
ROGER	Electric chair?

DICK   Wrong again.

            (*Beat.*)

ROGER   I'm stumped.

DICK   That, old son, is the original tranquilliser.
            That's where the word comes from. They
            used to use them for tranquillising the
            mutton-heads. Put 'em in, strap 'em up.

ROGER   Oh, nice. What do *you* want it for?

DICK   I'm gonna polish it up a bit, put a couple of
            pieces of wood on the bottom, make a nice
            rocker. A very nice rocking chair for the deck
            of my boat.

ROGER   Oh, nice one.

DICK   Take a gander in the sales-room sometime.
            They're selling all this stuff off. They've got
            some wonderful bargains. Some lovely
            Victorian knick-knacks.

TILLY   Can I talk to you, please?

DICK   Oh that part's gone, love.

TILLY   I've got a proposition to make.

DICK   (*to* ROGER) Ooh, propositioning us now, is
            she?

TILLY   Are you interested?

DICK   Are we interested? (*He looks at* LUKE *and*
            ROGER. *They shrug.*) We might be.

TILLY   I want to make a protest.

DICK   We're listening.

TILLY   On behalf of my friend Flo and all the other
            patients here. I want the public at large to
            know what's going on. About how we're
            being thrown out of our home and onto the
            streets.

DICK   Yeah, dreadful mess. And highly dangerous.

TILLY	(*firmer*) I want to be a human torch.
DICK	A what?
TILLY	I want to set fire to myself. I want you to film me.
	(*Beat.* DICK *is open-mouthed.*)
LUKE	Good God.
ROGER	That's a bit sick, isn't it?
	(*Beat.*)
DICK	Hang on, I must have a lump of wax in my ear because I don't think I could have heard you right. (*He puts his finger in his ear and wiggles it about.*) Right. That's better. Now then — come again?
TILLY	I want to be a human torch — and I want you to help me get it on film.
DICK	That's funny, I'm still hearing the same thing. (*He puts a finger in his other ear and wiggles that about.*)
TILLY	To be shown on "News at Ten".
	(*Beat.*)
LUKE	You *are* pulling our legs?
	(DICK, LUKE *and* ROGER *look at each other.*)
TILLY	If I leave here, my days are numbered, anyway. This way I could do some good. My death would be a way of giving meaning to my life.
LUKE	She's not taking the piss.
TILLY	I'm absolutely serious.
	(*Beat.*)
ROGER	You're mad.
TILLY	Yeah, I know.

LUKE	Let's hear her out, yeah? If she were a Buddhist monk we'd think she was saintly.
DICK	But people do not go around setting fire to themselves in this day and age.
TILLY	Can you get me on "News at Ten"?
	(*Beat.*)
LUKE	(*referring to* DICK) What colour's his tie?
TILLY	Sickly green.
LUKE	(*to* DICK) She seems rational enough.
DICK	Let me get this straight. You are saying you want to ... torch yourself ... and you want us to get it on the telly?
TILLY	As a protest.
DICK	As a protest. I have got that right?
TILLY	Absolutely right. To draw attention to my cause.
	(*Beat.* DICK *looks at* LUKE. *He looks at* ROGER. *He looks at* TILLY.)
DICK	Okay, so what's the punchline?
TILLY	What?
DICK	Well this is obviously some kind of stunt. So where's it leading? What are you after?
TILLY	I've told you. I want to awaken public opinion.
LUKE	So where do we come in?
TILLY	I want you to show me how to work the camera.
DICK	Oh, that's all, is it?
TILLY	Yes.
DICK	In other words, you want us to be accomplices in a serious crime?

TILLY	Suicide is not a crime. I just want you to show me how to work the camera and then turn a blind eye and leave the rest to me. You wouldn't have to get involved in any way.
DICK	Oh, I see. Well, that's some consolation, isn't it? So all we have to do is walk out the room, leaving you alone, come back and find you burned to a crisp? Magic. Is that the idea?
TILLY	Yes.
DICK	(*shaking his head*) Now what in God's name makes you think that we would go along with such a crazy bloody piece of nonsense?
TILLY	Well, I thought it would be good for all of us. I would get publicity for my cause and you'd get a lot of publicity for your company. You were saying yourself, before, that you haven't got any work, after this.
DICK	What, you heard all that?
TILLY	Yes, I was sitting in the corner. Over there.
DICK	What a ruddy cheek. Is there nowhere private in this place?
TILLY	No. And it occurred to me that this might be a good solution to *your* problems, too. You'd be interviewed on the telly, get your face and your company's name in the papers and magazines and so on. I'm sure all the publicity would help you get a lot of work.
	(*Pause.* DICK *looks at her searchingly.*)
DICK	Could you withdraw for a moment, so's I can have a little conflab with my colleagues?
TILLY	Oh, yes. Certainly. (*She exits.*)
DICK	Well ... blow me. What do you make of that, then?
LUKE	Out of the frame.

DICK   Bloody unbelievable. Eh? Absurd. Absolutely
              incredible.

ROGER   This is a loony-bin, isn't it?

DICK   Well the balance of her mind is certainly
              disturbed, there's no question of that. That
              ain't normal behaviour, is it?

ROGER   Mad as a pancake.

DICK   I suppose life in a place like this can't be all
              that glamorous.

ROGER   Not exactly Torremolinos, is it?

DICK   Setting fire to her bloody self. Where does
              she think she is? This is Western Civilisation,
              not the bloody Himalayas.

ROGER   The filming has obviously gone to her head.
              She's got a taste for it. "News at
              Ten" . . . blimey.

DICK   It wouldn't only be on "News at Ten", old
              son. It'd be on the front page of every bloody
              paper in the country, I should think. People
              just do not do that sort of thing. Not in
              these . . . enlightened . . . days. (*Beat. He looks
              at* LUKE *and* ROGER.) Either of you thinking
              what I'm thinking?

              (ROGER *and* LUKE *look at each other.*)

ROGER   Tell us what you're thinking first.

              (*Beat.*)

DICK   Nah . . . ridiculous.

              (*Beat.*)

ROGER   Is it?

              (*Beat.*)

DICK   Isn't it?

ROGER   Can't say till we know what you're thinking,
               can we?

               (*Beat.*)

DICK   Front page of every paper in the country.
               "News at Ten" ...

               (*Beat.*)

               She's right. You realise what that would
               mean?

ROGER   Like she says, a bit of free publicity, certainly.

DICK   It would be bloody "incalculatable", the
               amount of good that would do us. We'd
               probably need bloody Pickfords to take away
               the lolly. Maybe this girl isn't as daft as she
               looks.

ROGER   Steady on, Guv'nor ...

DICK   Well, at the very least, it would get us in the
               public eye. Maybe then we'd get to do some
               decent promos for name-artistes. I'm talking
               Rod Stewart. I'm talking Bowie. I'm talking
               Madonna. We could finally move out of that
               tatty attic and into something on the ground
               floor. We could even get an office with a
               window. Maybe be able to move from the
               obscurity of Waterloo to the plushness of
               Wardour Street. I know it seems audacious
               but we'd finally be part of the real film
               world. (*To* LUKE.) You could get a nice,
               floppy suit and a pair of specs with those big
               pink frames, so people can see you coming.
               Just think — we might finally be able to get
               in to the Groucho Club, accepted as equals
               by all the other prats in Soho. I tell you, son,
               if we don't grasp the opportunity, it's curtains
               for us. The end of the line. Going nowhere.
               Up against the buffer. (*To* LUKE.) What about
               you, squire?

LUKE	No way. It's sick.
DICK	I agree with that.
LUKE	The very idea — it's obscene.
DICK	No two ways about it.
LUKE	Taking advantage of a poor, unbalanced individual. I'd never forgive myself.
DICK	Your conscience would prick. Only natural. Unless she was gonna do it, anyway. Now imagine that. She goes and does it, anyway, and there's no-one around to record it for "austerity". Now that's what I call truly "sick". That's what I call truly "obscene". Now, seen in that light, her little act of self-sacrifice seems to me to be ...
ROGER	Tempting. Very.
DICK	And just think — that kind of publicity wouldn't do your career any harm, would it? You want to make a feature. Well before you can make a feature, you've got to get noticed. We all know that. That's the name of the game.
LUKE	Yes, well ... not like this. It's disgusting.
DICK	Viewed in one way, yes, absolutely. But, viewed in another, it's the opportunity of a bloody lifetime.
LUKE	It's grotesque, even to think about it.
ROGER	It's a gift. We'd be stupid to pass this up. You don't get a stroke of luck like this every day.
LUKE	Look, there are publicity stunts and publicity stunts. This is something else.
DICK	Yes — and I'll tell you what that something is. It's a godsend, for *all* of us.
LUKE	It's inhuman.
DICK	It was her idea. She wants to do it.

LUKE   My God, do you realise what you're saying?
        You're talking about helping someone to take
        her own life.

DICK   I'm talking about helping someone achieve
        her end.

LUKE   The woman is obviously ill.

DICK   Of course she's ill. You think a sane person
        would propose what she's proposing? So, like
        everyone else, just because she's ill, you want
        to wash your hands of her?

LUKE   I didn't say that.

DICK   Well, off you go, then Pontius ... don't let
        me detain you. (*He turns away.*)

LUKE   I didn't say I don't want to help. I just ...

DICK   Anyway, you're probably right. You do
        someone a favour, it always backfires. The
        old Bill'd be down on us like a ton of bricks.

ROGER   What for?

DICK   Well, we'd be accessories, wouldn't we?

ROGER   To what — leaving a camera lying around?
        How was we to know what stunt she was
        gonna pull? Not mind-readers, are we?

DICK   Nah, forget it.

ROGER   Look ... never mind "forget it". I say "let's
        go for it." My job's on the line here. If our
        little company goes down the pan, Guv'nor,
        it's all right for you. You'll find something.
        But what about me? Me, who's served you
        loyally through thick and thin. Have a heart,
        Guv. I'm saying, this could be the making of
        us. This could mean work. Now where's the
        risk? I mean, there's only us three who know
        about it. And her. Well, she ain't gonna be
        saying nothing, is she? Risk, what you talking
        about? You could walk out there now and get

knocked down by a mini-cab. Risk. You've
always said yourself, Guv'nor: it's them as
grabs the plate as gets the meat. Am I right?
Or am I right?

(*Beat.* DICK *looks at* ROGER, *admiringly.*)

DICK   Incredible. I took him on as a school-leaver.
                He could hardly spell his own name. And did
                you hear that? What a wonderful speaker
                he's turned out to be. Makes me feel quite
                humble. You're right, Rog. You're bloody
                right, old son. This girl needs help. She's
                desperate. And when someone comes to me
                with a plea for help like this little girl, then
                I've got the strength of character to try and
                ruddy-well see it from her P.O.V. (*He goes to
                the door, opens it and brings* TILLY *in.*) Now,
                lovey—

TILLY   Mathilda, actually. Mathilda Armitage.

DICK   Oh, very nice. Now, then, Mathilda, love I'm
                all for granting your request and helping you
                in any way I can. But there's one party here
                who still has strongish reservations about
                giving you the "sucker" I know you're crying
                out for.

TILLY   (*moving to* LUKE, *quietly*) I have to do it. With
                or without your help. Someone has to say
                "enough is enough".

DICK   Oh, I see that very clearly, lovey.

TILLY   Please do it for me. Do it for all of us mental
                patients everywhere, I beg you. I'll go down
                on my knees if you want me to ...

                (*She is just about to go down on her knees when*
                DICK *stops her.*)

DICK   No, no, lovey, that won't be necessary. I saw
                enough of that in the ruddy Navy. (*He picks
                her up. To* LUKE.) Well, it's up to you, squire.
                It's do-we-or-don't we time. Do you want to
                make that feature?

(LUKE *paces, confused, struggling.* DICK *and* ROGER *move away.*)

LUKE (*to* TILLY) You do realise the seriousness of what you've proposed?

TILLY Yes. I do.

LUKE But bearing in mind the fact that you're . . .

TILLY Loopy?

LUKE Well . . .

TILLY Bananas?

LUKE Well, not exactly.

TILLY I'm fine. They wouldn't have released me if I wasn't, would they?

LUKE Well, no . . . I suppose not.

TILLY And the fact that I came back is further proof that I'm sane, don't you think?

LUKE How do you work that out?

TILLY Well, it would have been insane to stay out there. So anyone who comes back has *got* to be sane. The insane ones are the ones out there who think that's what sanity is. Only the *truly* sane know that that's *insane* and that people who put up with it must be *mad*. So anyone who's been in a place like this and come back again is not only sane but, to my way of thinking, *doubly* sane, because you must be mad if you think that the people in here are madder than the people out there because the people out there *claim* to be normal and that's *not* normal and the people in here who supposedly *aren't* normal *don't* claim to be normal at all. And that's a *far* more sane thing to do. Don't you think?

(*Beat.* LUKE *looks confused, defeated.*)

LUKE	Yes, I'm sure it is. But I just want to know that you realise it's . . . irreversible.
TILLY	Of course. Once it's done, that's it.
	(LUKE *looks at her for a moment.*)
LUKE	Good. Okay. That's the most important thing. (*To* DICK.) Okay, let's go for it.
DICK	(*smiling, to* TILLY) That's it, then, love, we're all batting for you.
TILLY	Thank you. Forgive me mentioning something so tasteless but . . . I was wondering if you could see your way to . . . making me a donation . . . so that I can settle my finances?
DICK	(*suspicious*) Oh yes? How much are we talking about, then?
TILLY	Well, I want to send my friend, Flo, off to Canada to see her daughter, Lilly, and her little baby. So we're talking about enough for the air-fare. And a perm and blow-dry. Five hundred pounds? (DICK *whistles.*)
DICK	(*turning away to hide his delight*) That's a lot of money.
ROGER	(*meaning it*) A lot of money. And, let's face it, we're not talking about a week's work here. We're talking about half-an-hour at the most. (DICK *looks at him aggressively.*) Oh, sorry. Sorry, Guv.
DICK	Cheque be all right, would it, covered by a banker's card?
TILLY	Oh, no, strictly cash, I'm afraid.
DICK	Oh. Right. Okay. Fine. No probs.
	(DICK *looks at* LUKE. *He nods.* ROGER *gives a discreet thumbs up.*)

And I think the least we can do is give you a wonderful send-off, slap-up meal, champagne, After Eights — no expense spared.

TILLY   Oh, that's very nice of you.

DICK   What do you fancy, love?

TILLY   Well, I'm going through a Chinese phase at the moment. There's a little place outside the Main Gate called the Eater's Digest. If you could ask for an Iron Rice Bowl. That's a special where you get a bit of everything thrown in. And two portions of special fried rice.

ROGER   One Iron Rice Bowl. And *two* portions of rice?

TILLY   (*half apologetic*) They don't feed us very well here. All the good food goes to the physically ill.

DICK   Well that'll probably *make* you physically ill, so no problem.

LUKE   And we'll need your signature on a piece of paper making clear that it was your decision entirely.

DICK   And that there was no "cohesion" applied.

TILLY   Oh, certainly — a suicide note.

DICK   (*attempting to lighten the atmosphere*) You'd have to leave it in a pre-arranged spot, of course. Somewhere not too close to the "epicentre" of where the event would take place. Wouldn't want that going up in smoke as well, would we? (*He laughs.*)

TILLY   Oh that's a good point, isn't it.

               (TILLY *laughs. They all join in. Suddenly,* DICK *stops.*)

DICK   We'll have to move quite sharpish. Dinner-
                time's the best bet, I reckon. We'll give you a
                little lesson in the rudiments of filming, pick
                a good spot for you to ... "self-marinate"
                yourself. Then we'll pop out for our meal,
                come back and there you'll be. Well ... were.
                (*He looks at* ROGER, *pulls a "slanty-eye".*) Off
                you go then, Roger.

ROGER   Oh, right.

                (ROGER *exits.* DICK *changes mood, moves close to*
                TILLY.)

DICK   You know, only the other day, one of my
                kiddies, the little one, she said to me:
                "Daddy, why are you in the entertainment
                industry?" And I said then and I'll say it until
                my dying day ...   (*He bends down and points a
                finger at a point about two and a half feet from the
                ground, as though talking to an imaginary child.*)
                "I'm in this game to make other people
                happy." There it is. It's as complex and as
                simple as that.

                (*Pause.*)

LUKE   And *I'd* just like to add that I understand that
                life is not easy for you people. And I
                understand some of your fears about the
                outside world. But I want you to know that
                there are people who *care* for your plight.
                That's why we're going along with this. To
                make people remember. Lest they forget. I
                think that speaks volumes, so I'll say no
                more.

                (*Lights fade.*)

                            Scene Two

                Later. TILLY *stands waiting as* DICK *lays a
                tablecloth on a little table and sets it for* TILLY'S
                meal.

                ROGER *enters, carrying two plastic carrier bags.*

DICK   Right, let's get this all set up, then. We
                haven't got much time.

                (ROGER *holds up the bags.* DICK *takes them and
                takes out the After Eights.*)

                Here we are, love ... one Chinky-Chinese.
                Plus a packet of After-Eights and ... (*He
                takes out a bottle of champagne.*) ... a bottle of
                champagne, as per promise.

TILLY   Oh, that's very considerate but I don't drink
                alcohol, thank you very much.

DICK   (*looking at* ROGER, *cheesed off*) Why didn't you
                check that out before you spent the money,
                you big glob of gunge?

TILLY   You have it.

DICK   Right.

                (TILLY *moves forward to grab the food but* DICK
                pulls it out of her way.)

                Oh, let's get that note written, first, shall we?
                Sit down, love. Roger ...

ROGER   Yes, Guv?

DICK   Furnish the girl with pen and paper.

ROGER   Right, Guv.

                (TILLY *sits.* ROGER *hands* TILLY *a pad of paper
                and a pen.*)

DICK   Try and make it as legible as you can, lovey.
                As though you were sitting an exam. Nice
                and neat.

TILLY   Right. I'll try. (*She starts to write.*)

LUKE   (*entering*) How's it going?

DICK   Everything's progressing according to plan.
                (*Whispering to* LUKE.) Why don't you stay here
                and watch her for a moment and we'll slip
                out and get the rest of the gear?

LUKE   Oh ... do I have to?

            (DICK *and* ROGER *exit.*)

TILLY   Just writing my farewell note.

LUKE   Ah. Good. (LUKE *is uncomfortable. He doesn't know what to say.*) Look, I'm sorry about the cock-up this morning.

TILLY   Oh, that's all right. That's all behind us now.

LUKE   Sometimes in this business you've really got to think on your feet. It can be bloody tough. Naturally, I'm not saying it's as tough as it is for you out there, say, but ... it's got its downside, I can assure you. That's why I'm hoping that the little piece we're ... doing together later will help put my name around a bit. I've put so many good ideas forward to Channel Four over the years but without success. I *did* have a *great* idea for a cookery series. To be called Celebrity Kitchens. The idea was that each week we'd visit a different celebrity in their kitchen. Obviously. But they sat on that for eighteen months and then threw it back at me. They said: "what's the point? You'd only end up with Barbara Windsor and Lionel Blair." That's what's wrong with this industry these days. Everything you try to do, you end up with Lionel Blair. It's very dispiriting.

TILLY   Yes, I can imagine.

            (DICK *enters, carrying camera equipment.* LUKE *is much relieved.*)

LUKE   Well, I'd better press on. See you later.

TILLY   Yes, okay.

            (LUKE *exits.* DICK *watches* TILLY *write for a moment and moves in and stares over her shoulder. She notices. He speaks more out of embarrassment than anything else.*)

DICK	(*suddenly*) How long were you in this place, love? How long was your sentence?
TILLY	Oh, I wasn't sentenced. It's not like a prison. I didn't do anything wrong.
DICK	No, 'course not, I er . . .
TILLY	I had a nervous breakdown.
DICK	That so?
TILLY	Yeah. On account of what happened to my babies.
DICK	Oh. You have children, do you?
TILLY	I think about my babies all the time. They're grown up now.
DICK	Oh yes? Where are they?
TILLY	Well this is it, you see. I got ever-so-ill, after my mother died. I got such terrible depression. She was lovely woman. Kindest woman you ever met. She was all I had. My dad ran off when I was a child. He was a seaman. Just like my husband. Now you see him, now you don't. Me and my mum, we coped all right but then, when my mother died . . . (*She bends her head.*) I couldn't cope. I thought God was so cruel to take her. I stopped going out of the house. Couldn't bear to think of shopping or anything like that. I started living in my own world. I imagined everyone was trying to take my babies away from me. (*Pause.*) They used to cry all the time from hunger, but I was too scared to go out in case people took them away from me. And one day . . . they were crying so much — 'cos they were so hungry, the poor little loves — that I thought we'd all be better off together in heaven, with my mum. So I mixed up all the asprin I had and I gave it to them. But there wasn't enough

for me as well. So I had to slash my wrists.
But it made me scream so much with the
pain that the neighbours broke the door
down.

DICK   What ... what happened to the kiddies, love?

TILLY   They said I tried to murder them. But it's
not true. I never meant to harm them. I just
wanted to put them out of their misery. I was
ill. They put me away and ... I had to let
them go. That's a sadness in my life, what
happened to my babies.

(*Pause.* DICK *shakes his head, genuinely moved.*)

DICK   Certainly makes you think, a tale like that.
(*He looks at the note. He speaks more out of a
feeling of inadequacy than anything else.*) That
ready? Go on, then. Read it out to me, love.

TILLY   "I Mathilda Armitage, do this as a protest at
the way I have been treated. We patients are
being discharged from our homes without
proper help being given to us, forcing us to
live like tramps in private madhouses or like
vagrants on the streets of our once-great
land. I wish you all a fond farewell. I have no
regrets. Ta-ta."

DICK   (*genuinely sympathetic*) Very nice. I like that,
very much. There's poetry in there. (*He takes
the note and looks at it.*) You know, I think I'm
gonna photocopy this and put a copy on the
wall of my little cottage in the country.

(ROGER *enters carrying a blank video cassette
which he holds up.*)

DICK   Good. Right. Let's press on. You tuck into
that meal, love, and we'll get all the doings
ready.

TILLY   (*moving towards the door*) Okay. I just need to
get my pram and wash my hands.

DICK   That's hardly necessary, love.

TILLY   No, I mean ... *wash my hands*, you
            know ... in the other sense.

DICK   *Other* sense?

TILLY   You know, in the sense of *not* washing them.

DICK   Eh ... ?

TILLY   In the sense of having a *pee*. I need to *piss*.

DICK   Oh, right. Fair enough.

TILLY   I'll just have a quick splash and I'll be
            straight back.

DICK   Right. Yeah. Don't be too long, though,
            lovey. Time is of the essence.

TILLY   I won't be a jiff. I think it's nerves stretching
            my bladder.

DICK   Yeah, sure. Er ... you go right ahead, love.
            (TILLY *exits*.) What's the point of relieving
            yourself before you ... ? Cor blimey, human
            nature.

ROGER   Maybe she thought she might put the fire
            out. If she ... you know ... *went*, on the
            spot. (DICK *looks at him in disgust*.)

DICK   What a sick imagination you've got.

            (*Beat.* ROGER *takes out the Chinese meal*.)

ROGER   An hour from now she'll feel like another
            one of these Chinese meals. (*Beat*.) Well, she
            would normally. But not on this occasion, eh?
            (*He laughs. He pours the champagne*.) Wants to
            leave her mark, eh? Well, she'll certainly do
            that, won't she?

            (ROGER *hands a paper cup to* DICK, *who shakes
            his head at* ROGER'S *insensitivity*.)

            Let's toast her, shall we? Here's to the success
            of our venture. (*He raises his paper cup*.)

DICK   Was that deliberate?

ROGER   What?

DICK   "Let's toast her."

            (*It dawns on* ROGER.)

ROGER   Oh. Oops. Sorry. (*He laughs.*)

            (*They drink. Pause.*)

DICK   You know, it's quite touching.

ROGER   What's that, Guv?

DICK   She's had a tough life, that kid.

            (ROGER *brings over two cans of petrol.*)

ROGER   Two cans be enough, d'you reckon?

DICK   Two cans? Are you out of your mind?
            There's enough there to firebomb Dresden.
            All she'll need is a gallon or two. Put the
            other out of harm's way. She'll burn the
            bloody place down if we're not careful.

            (ROGER *takes a can back.*)

ROGER   Yeah, we should put down a plastic sheet or
            something for her to sit on.

DICK   A plastic sheet? What the bloody hell do you
            think's gonna happen to a *plastic* sheet?

ROGER   Oh.

DICK   We need metal, something like that.

ROGER   We could shove her on a bed?

DICK   Yeah. Great for the first ten minutes but
            what happens when she keels over? We're
            gonna have all the ... gubbins dropping
            through the springs onto the floor. No, we
            need something sturdy.

            (DICK *paces, looking for something suitable.*
            ROGER *holds up the brass dedication plaque.*)

ROGER   He'are, she can sit on this.

DICK   Oh, you dick-head.

ROGER   What's up?

DICK   You see what's on the other side of that?

ROGER   No. (*He turns it around.*) "In memory of Dr Elias Shadwell ... " Oh yeah?

DICK   I was gonna take that home and put it in my conservatory, you bollock. You're gonna ruin it ...

ROGER   It'll be all right. I'll give it a going-over with Brasso when she's finished. It'll come up a treat.

DICK   Well, if there's nothing else, all right, come on. (ROGER *puts the plaque on the floor*.) We've got to make sure everything's all right for her. Don't want some busybody trooping in when she's half-done, putting her out. The bugger is we don't know how slowly or how quickly she's going to ... combust. I mean, she may go up like a torch or she may hang around smouldering for hours.

ROGER   Blimey, that's a thought.

DICK   I want it to be as painless as possible for the poor girl.

   (TERRY *enters, angry and aggressive, shouting*.)

TERRY   They keep feeding me food but I'm not Henry the Eighth! I'm not Henry the fucking eighth!

   (ROGER *goes towards* TERRY, *shooing him out like a chicken*.)

ROGER   Go on, shoo. Outside.

DICK   Go on, off you pop. (*To* ROGER.) The bugger doesn't know which way up he is. Show him your elbows.

ROGER   (*rolling up his sleeves, as a warning*) Go on, off
             you trot! This is private property. Out!

TERRY   (*getting the message*) All right, I'm going. Yes
             — I'm off to spend the rest of the day
             amongst people with more reasonable
             haircuts!

ROGER   (*pointing a finger at* TERRY) Don't you play
             silly buggers with me, I'm warning you.

TERRY   (*standing up to him*) You know, I always
             thought you were a man with a quiff.

ROGER   What?

TERRY   Yes, I've always thought that about you.

ROGER   (*perplexed, irritated*) What do you mean, you
             always thought I was a man with a quiff?

             (*They stare at each other uneasily for a moment.*)

TERRY   I hope you don't mind my saying this but I
             think you should wear your hair curly.

ROGER   What?

TERRY   Yes, I think so.

ROGER   You taking the piss? You ... (*He lightly hits*
             TERRY *on the chest.*)

DICK: Take it easy.

ROGER: What's he trying to do — make a berk out of
             me?

DICK   Leave him, what does it matter?

ROGER   (*getting more and more angry*) I want to know
             what he means! He's not saying this for
             nothing. It's some kind of code. Come on,
             tell me what you're driving at!

TERRY   Yes, some sort of quiff, definitely.

ROGER   Explain yourself. (*He grabs* TERRY *and throws*
             him to the floor.) Tell me why you keep saying
             these things to me.

DICK   Get off him, you bloody maniac!

TERRY   Help! Help!

ROGER   (*shaking* TERRY *violently*) Tell me! Tell me!

TERRY   Ugh! Ugh!

DICK   Have you gone out of your mind?

                (DICK *rushes to* ROGER, *grabs him off* TERRY *and
                throws* ROGER *aside.* TERRY *staggers back,
                clutching his throat.*)

                You bloody lunatic, what's the matter with
                you?

ROGER   He's been needling me ever since we came
                here. Saying things to me that he knows I
                can't work out. Nasty things. Codes,
                messages. Trying to make me feel bad!
                Trying to upset me!

                (DICK *runs towards* TERRY. TERRY *makes for the
                door, hastily.*)

DICK   Go on, get out of here, you bloody nuisance.

                (TERRY *rushes out.*)

ROGER   He knows what he's doing. People like that,
                they make me sick. It's a smokescreen, all this
                bizarre bit. He's just a lazy good-for-nothing.
                He's not the crazy one. We're the bleeding
                nut-cases for putting up with it.

DICK   You silly sod, you're going to ruin the whole
                enterprise.

ROGER   I'm sorry, I must be overwrought.

                (ROGER *takes a cigarette out of his pocket, strikes a
                match. He is sitting next to the petrol can.*)

DICK   (*jumping back, terrified*) What are you doing?

ROGER   I need a fag.

DICK   You'll blow us all to kingdom-come, you
                bloody dimwit!

                (ROGER *looks at his cigarette and then at the
                lighted match. Then he notices the petrol and
                jumps back, too, putting the match out as he does.*)

ROGER   God Almighty. I'm sorry. I don't know what
                got into me.

                (TILLY *enters, pushing her pram.*)

DICK   Ah, there she is, the girl herself.

TILLY   I've invited my friend Flo to come in and say
                "goodbye".

DICK   You haven't said anything about ... ? (*He
                points to the petrol cans.*)

TILLY   No, of course not.

DICK   And you haven't invited anyone else, I hope?
                This isn't bonfire night, you know.

TILLY   No, only Flo. (TILLY *goes to the table and sits.
                She and* ROGER *unpack the food.*) Oh, I've been
                thinking and dreaming about Chinese food
                for months.

DICK   Well you just tuck in and enjoy yourself, love.

                (*Beat. Suddenly* TILLY *looks at* ROGER *sternly.*)

TILLY   You forgot the spring rolls.

DICK   You what?

TILLY   (*disappointed*) He forgot the spring rolls.

DICK   You forgot the spring rolls for the girl, you
                big lump of lard!

ROGER   Oh. Sorry. I thought ... Well, blimey!
                There's enough food there to choke a horse.

DICK   Button it, you ponce. (*To* TILLY.) He can
                always rush back for them, if you're
                desperate. (*He looks at his watch nervously.*)

TILLY   Oh, it doesn't matter. I'm sure I can get some
                when I get to ... you know ... (*She looks up
                at the sky.*) Where I'm going.

                (DICK *and* ROGER *look heavenwards, too. Then
                they look down.*)

DICK   Let's hope so, lovey. Let's hope so.

                (*Quick Fade.*)

                ## Scene Three

                *The same, later. The lights, camera, etc, are now
                all trained on the brass plaque, which is laid out
                on the floor, ready for filming.*

                TILLY *stands next to the camera as* DICK *shows
                her how to operate it.*

DICK   That's the only thing you have to press, the
                red record button. Nothing else. It's all fully-
                automatic.

LUKE   Think you can manage that?

TILLY   Yes, I'm sure I can, thank you.

DICK   (*walking her towards the plaque*) Then you park
                yourself down on this nice piece of brass.
                (*Pointing to the petrol.*) The ... liquid's right
                there. The matches, likewise. You may feel
                you want to slip your woolly off, lovey, just to
                speed things up a little. It looks a bit thick.
                (*He helps her off with her cardigan.*) So, any
                questions?

TILLY   No. I think that's all I need to know.

DICK   Well, that's everything set up. When you've
                said your farewells to your friend, we'll slip
                out quietly for our supper, just the other side
                of that door there, and I think you can go for
                a take any time you feel ready.

TILLY	(*nervous*) Right, okay.
DICK	You're shaking like a leaf.
TILLY	I'm a bit nervous.
DICK	Well, that's understandable. You know, if it's any consolation, lovey, apparently it's such a shock to the system that the body's natural defence-mechanism takes over and cuts out all pain. This is why, in the East, they've been doing it for centuries. It's part of their customs, they think nothing of it. A very popular way of going. It's clean. It's tidy. And it's memorable.
TILLY	Yes, I believe so. Anyway, I know I'm in capable hands.
LUKE	You said it. Capable hands. That's a nice image.

(ROGER *brings over a fire extinguisher, which he holds up, proudly in front of* TILLY.)

DICK	There we are. I just want you to know, lovey, that should you change your mind, should you call out to stop, there's (*he reads the label*) forty-four-pounds-per-square-inch of foam there that's gonna be coming to your rescue. You might get a bit wet but . . . we'll put you out.
TILLY	Thank you, that's very considerate of you.
DICK	Right, let's get on with it. Hand over the money, Roger, and let her say her farewells.

(ROGER *hands* TILLY *five hundred pounds.*)

ROGER	It's all there. Count it, if you like.
TILLY	I'm not in the mood for counting. Anyway, I'm sure you wouldn't lie to me.

(ROGER *goes to the door, peers through it.*)

ROGER	She's here, Guv, the peculiar one. Shall I let her in?
DICK	Yes. Just a mo'. (*To* TILLY.) We'll slip back to say our own farewells once you've said goodbye.
TILLY	That would be nice.
DICK	And if you could be fairly quick about it, love. Time's running a bit short.
TILLY	I understand.

(ROGER *opens the door for* FLO *and she enters as* DICK *exits with* ROGER *and* LUKE.)

TILLY	(*loud, as they exit*) How are the spiders, Flo?
FLO	What spiders?

(TILLY *closes the door behind them and then checks that the doors are closed. Suddenly, her character changes. She becomes more animated. She takes out the money and flicks through it happily.*)

TILLY	(*in a loud whisper*) Oh, doesn't matter. I've been a bit naughty — look.
FLO	Where did you get that from?
TILLY	Off the film people.
FLO	Good God, you haven't been selling something you shouldn't?
TILLY	No. I conned it off them.
FLO	No. How?

(*Beat.* TILLY *looks towards the doors to make sure nobody is listening.*)

TILLY	I told them I was going to set fire to myself.
FLO	You what?
TILLY	Set myself on fire.
FLO	Oh my God, whatever for?

TILLY   (*suddenly stern*) Five hundred pounds, that's
             what for. That'll get me through the winter.

             (TILLY *goes to her pram and quickly begins to take
             things off it and wrap them in plastic bags.*)

FLO   Oh, Tilly, you'll get yourself into trouble.
             They could have you arrested.

TILLY   Oh, that'd be terrible, wouldn't it? They'd
             have me sent straight back here. They'd have
             to give me three square meals a day and a
             nice bed for the night. That'd be a disaster.

FLO   But what did you want to go and say
             something like that for?

TILLY   They treated me like a toe-rag, Flo. Nobody
             tells me to do basket-weaving and gets away
             with it!

FLO   Oh, they made a mistake taking you on, Till.

TILLY   Had a few tricky moments but, as you know,
             I've always had good expressions.

FLO   You *could* have been Prime Minister with a
             bit of make-up. I've always said that about
             you.

TILLY   Now I've got to scarper, sharpish.

FLO   Yes, you'd better get a move on.

TILLY   I'm going to have to leave my pram. Once I
             get outside the grounds, I'm going to have to
             run like the clappers. We've done a lot of
             miles together. You have it, Flo. I know you'll
             take care of it.

FLO   Oh, that's kind of you, Tilly. (*Unsure.*) But
             where will you go?

TILLY   Back to the seaside. Where else? (*She removes
             a bundle of notes and hands them to* FLO.) That's
             for you. There's about fifty quid there.

FLO	What? Oh, I couldn't take that.
TILLY	Yes, you can. You spend it on whatever you fancy.
FLO	Oh, no. You need it yourself, Tilly.
TILLY	You take it. You helped me to get it, Flo.
FLO	Me? How?
TILLY	Oh, I haven't got time to explain. But I couldn't have done it without you. Keep it, you earned it. (*Pressing it firmly into* FLO's *hand.*) Now I've got to dash. Ta-ta, Flo. I hope we see each other again, sometime.
FLO	So do I, Till. Goodbye and God bless, love.

(*They embrace quickly.* TILLY *rushes to the window. She pushes the window but it's locked.*)

TILLY	Oh blimey!
FLO	What's the matter?
TILLY	I can't get the windows open. They're all sealed.

(*She tries another, then another.*)

FLO	Oh dear.
TILLY	Oh, Gordon Bennett! (*Putting her bags down.*) Look, Flo ... I've got to do some quick-thinking here. Look ... (*Taking the money out of her coat.*) Take this and hide it behind the garden sheds. In the hole in the wall. Then get Georgie and come back here as quick as you can.
FLO	Hole in the wall ... then Georgie. But what about you — how are you going to get out?
TILLY	I'll think of something.

(TILLY *puts her two bags in* FLO's *hands and gives her the pram and then escorts her to the door. She opens the door and* FLO *goes out as* DICK *and* ROGER *enter, followed by* LUKE.)

DICK   Everything all right, love?

TILLY   Yes, fine, thank you. I've just given Flo some
              of my old possessions. And my dear old
              pram.

DICK   So I see. A nice gesture, lovey. Very
              thoughtful.

              (DICK *and* ROGER *and* LUKE *stand in front of*
              TILLY *so that she cannot get out. They walk*
              forwards, towards the camera. TILLY *is nervous*
              but controlled.)

TILLY   You known I've been thinking: they mightn't
              like to show me ... you know — actually
              burning, on the telly. They have rules about
              that kind of thing, don't they? Family viewing
              and all that. They might find it a bit tasteless.

DICK   No — plane crashes, pile-ups, serial killings,
              this is the kind of thing they go in for these
              days. I think you're wrong. I think they'll like
              it very much.

TILLY   (*playing for time*) But ... just in case ... I
              think it might be a good idea if we were
              to ... do a bit of filming beforehand. You
              know, me telling the viewers why I'm doing
              it. That kind of thing.

ROGER   Nah, I don't think they'd be that interested,
              would they?

              (DICK *looks at his watch.*)

DICK   (*halting* ROGER) Well ... perhaps a few words
              of explanation wouldn't a bad idea.

LUKE   A sort of *filmic* suicide note? That's good.

TILLY   Yeah. Could we have a go, d'you think? Have
              you got enough film in the camera?

DICK   It's video these days, love. Marvellous. Half-
              an-hour, non-stop.

TILLY Oh, even *I* couldn't talk for that long — and I can talk the legs off a donkey.

LUKE You say it however you think fit. These will, indeed, be famous last words.

(TILLY *sits on the table.* DICK *and* ROGER *quickly clear it for her.* LUKE *trains the camera on her.*)

TILLY I think I'll be here. Can you get me from this angle, d'you think?

DICK Any way you choose, lovey, we are here to serve.

TILLY I don't really have a best side, you see, but I worry a bit about my double chin.

(*They form a crew behind the camera and turn it on.*)

DICK How's the light?

LUKE No problem. She's looking good.

DICK (*looking through the lens*) Oh, very nice, Tilly, love. You'll like this. Very breakfast-TV.

TILLY How's my hair?

DICK Tip top, love.

LUKE Couldn't be better.

TILLY Right. I'm ready. (*To* LUKE.) Immortalise me!

ROGER (*shouting*) Okay, settle down everybody. Going for a take.

(DICK *looks at him.*)

LUKE Right, then. Roger — turn over.

(ROGER *turns the camera on.*)

ROGER Running ...

(LUKE *mimes banging a clapper-board.*)

LUKE "Slate missing" — take one. And ... action.

(TILLY *doesn't move.*)

DICK   Action. That's you, love. Go on.

TILLY   Good evening, viewers. My name is Tilly
            Armitage. Thank you for turning on to
            "News at Ten". You don't know me. Well,
            some of you might. Those who live around
            Hastings or the Southampton and
            Portsmouth way. These are all places I have
            frequented in my travels. A lot of you will
            have seen me cat-napping in a deckchair on
            the pier. Or kipping in the library. You may
            even have caught me asleep in your doorway
            as you came out to take in the early-morning
            milk.

DICK   Try and keep it snappy, love.

            (*During this speech* TILLY *warms up and gets into
            her stride, becoming more and more passionate
            until, at the end, it is a real battle-cry, with her
            seeming more "unbalanced" than she has so far.*)

TILLY   Oh, right. Well ... the point is, I'm out there
            now and out there belongs to me as much as
            to you 'cos that's where I come from. And
            you lot are going to have to get used to
            having us around. So I just want to tell you
            to knock it off, all that spitting at us and
            giving us a hard time. Throwing us out of
            cafés, mocking us in the streets. All right, so
            some of us are a bit peculiar. But we've had a
            lot of good people in our ranks. A lot of
            genius-like people over the years. Saints,
            sinners, politicians, royalty, inventors,
            composers, artists of all sorts ... chiropodists.
            They've all done their bit, all had their part
            to play. And you just remember, you
            wouldn't have had any electric light if it
            hadn't been for a madman. You wouldn't
            have had any telephones to talk on. Or motor
            cars or aeroplanes. Or saints to look up to.
            Or great books to read or wonderful music to
            listen to. Or leaders to win your wars or

politicians to make your laws. So whenever
you see someone who's depressed or
deranged, personality-disordered,
schizophrenic, manic-depressive, psychotic,
hallucinating . . . if you come across someone
who believes in miracles, U.F.Os, the flat-
earth, energetic-engineering, faith-healing,
potato-peeling, crime-doesn't-pay, March
follows May . . . give that person the time of
day! And enough for a cup of tea. Yeah . . . I
think that's all. I think that'll do . . .

(The camera crew, who have been following TILLY
everywhere, all fall down. TILLY *looks nervously
towards the door.)*

LUKE   *(quietly, sincerely)* Very nice, Tilly.

ROGER   Bit long, though.

DICK   A bit of editing and that could make a nice
            little feature.

TILLY   You sure you got all that?

ROGER   It's all in the can, no worries.

TILLY   And you'll see to it that it gets on "News at
            Ten"?

DICK   You leave that to me, love. I know some very
            powerful people in the TV industry.

            *(*GEORGIE *enters, with* FLO *following.)*

GEORGIE   What's going on, what's the problem?

TILLY   Oh, thank God, Georgie, where've you been?

FLO   It's them.

TILLY   I'll be off now, then.

LUKE   What . . . ?

DICK   What do you mean, "off"?

TILLY   I'm just about to leave for the seaside. Like I
            was ordered to. Wasn't I, Georgie?

(TILLY *makes for the door.* DICK *and the crew are amazed, confused.* DICK *runs to* TILLY, *gently holds her arm.*)

DICK   I think we need you for a bit more filming, don't we?

TILLY   Oh, no, I think I've made my point. I think that's enough.

LUKE   I don't think it is.

TILLY   Oh yes — I think you'll find it is.

GEORGIE   Will somebody please explain to me what's going on?

TILLY   I have to pop off now or I'll never get back. Gosh, is that the time? If I don't go now, I'll miss my train.

LUKE   (*realising*) Oh Christ! (*He turns away from the group.*)

DICK   Oh, my good God Almighty! (DICK *walks away from them.*)

ROGER   (*angry*) In that case, we'll have our money back.

GEORGIE   What's this?

ROGER   Money that the Guv'nor was kind enough to lend her out of the goodness of his heart. We'll have it back, then.

              (DICK *sits, his mind reeling.*)

GEORGIE   Is this true, Tilly? Have you borrowed money from these gentlemen?

ROGER   She must think we was born yesterday.

DICK   Shut up.

ROGER   Diabolical bloody liberty.

DICK   Enough, you pillock!

              (*Silence.*)

GEORGIE	You must return what you borrowed.
TILLY	No, I won't. They only gave it to me because they thought I was going to ... (*She moves forward and steps onto the plaque.*)
DICK	All right! All right. Let's call it a long story that's not worth the re-telling. I'm not a vindictive man. You keep the money. (DICK *turns away.*)
GEORGIE	I think Mr. Headley deserves a 'thank you,' don't you, Tilly?
TILLY	(*cocky, playful*) Thank you very much, Mr. Headley. Much appreciated, I'm sure.
GEORGIE	Well, that's settled. (*Looking at his watch.*) Tilly, pop by my office on your way out and say goodbye.
TILLY	Right, Georgie ...
	(GEORGIE *exits.* TILLY *goes to her pram and pushes it towards the door.*)
DICK	(*calling to her*) I've been a right bloody chump, haven't I?
LUKE	Haven't we all ... ?
	(TILLY *stops pushing her pram, turns and comes back to the group.*)
TILLY	Don't feel too bad. You're not the first punters I've taken for a ride. You have to be a bit of an actress on the streets, these days. To get by.
LUKE	A remarkable performance. No question of that.
TILLY	(*delighted*) Oh, thank you. Perhaps if ever you need someone of my particular skills and calibre, you could come down and visit my chalet sometime? I'm right on the sea-front. There's a row of blue beach-huts. I'm

number forty seven. Just knock on the door, anytime. I can usually hear. I live underneath.

LUKE   (*half-amused*) Thank you, I'll bear it in mind.

(DICK *looks at* TILLY, *shakes his head.*)

DICK   How could I have been such a wally ... ?

TILLY   (*crossing to him*) Don't tell me you've never been tapped by an ex-mental patient before?

DICK   (*outraged at the suggestion*) No, I bloody-well haven't!

TILLY   Well, you'd better get used to it! Because there's hundreds of thousands of us. And we're coming.

(TILLY *turns to walk towards her pram and the door.*)

Blackout.

PROPS LIST

ACT ONE

On Stage

Park Bench
Statue of Lord Shaftesbury
Grass Roller
Tractor Furrow Blade

Off Stage

Canvas Director's Chair (Roger)
Dedication Plaque (Dick)
Handkerchief (Dick)
Manuscript (Luke)
Camera (Luke)
Clipboard, Pen (Roger)
2 Plastic Carrier Bags with Clothing (Tilly)
Pram (Tilly)
Small Table (Roger)
Breakfast on Tray (Roger)
Coins (Terry)
4 Cigars (Dick)
Electrical Cables
Electric Boxes
Camera Stands
Ladder
Paint Pots, Brushes
Bits of Wood and Scaffolding
Bag (Flo) Containing:
    Knitting
    Photograph
Photo, Pen (Jok)
Watch (Luke)
Kitchen Knife (Terry)
Hand Mirror (Jok)
Briefcase with Paperwork (Dick)
Mannequins
Walkie Talkie (Roger)
Straight Jacket (Jok)
Sunglasses (Jok)
Megaphone (Luke)

ACT TWO

On Stage

Tea Urn and Tea Cups
Chair
Newspaper
Exercise Horse
Video Camera and Stand
Large Book
Electrical Cables from Act One
Electric Boxes from Act One
Table
Dick's Briefcase
Mannequins from Act One
Fire Extinguisher

Off Stage

Clip-board (Roger)
Dedication Plaque from Act One (Roger)
2 Cans of Petrol (Roger)
Wad of Money (Dick)
Restraining Chair with Straps (Dick)
Watch (Dick)
Tablecloth (Dick)
Placesetting (Dick)
2 Carrier Bags (Roger) Containing:
   Champagne
   After Eight Mints
   Paper Cups
   Chinese Takeaway Meal
Paper, Pen (Roger)
Blank Video Cassette (Roger)
Cigarettes, Matches (Roger)
£500 Pounds (Roger)

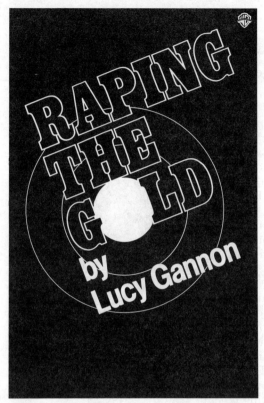

Set on and around an archery field in a small Derbyshire town beset by the closure of the local factory works, the metaphor of an arrow splitting the golden centre of an archer's target emphasizes the way in which long term unemployment shatters the dreams and ideas of a community torn apart by events beyond their control.

This powerful and moving play contrasts the hopes and despair of friends and family within the community, uncompromising in their personal beliefs. *Raping The Gold*'s warm sense of humour is complemented by a fierce compassion for individuals whose lives are caught between a betrayed past and an abandoned future, where for some the local archery club is the only source of solace and inspiration left available.

"It is a work of outstanding talent." *Sunday Times*

"Ms Gannon has a powerful sense of place and mood ... Her great gift is the capacity to convey desolation through resonant images." *The Guardian*

For further information contact Warner Chappell Plays Ltd, 129 Park Street, London W1Y 3FA. Telephone 01-629-7600.

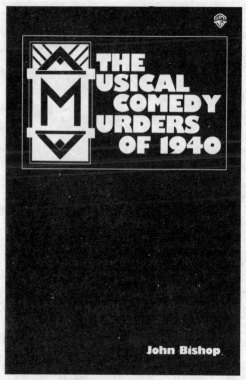

THE MUSICAL COMEDY MURDERS OF 1940

John Bishop

Under the guise of a backer's audition for their new musical, the production team of a recent Broadway flop assemble at an isolated country mansion to try to piece together the identity of the mysterious "Stage Door Slasher", who murdered three of the chorus girls in the show. While a blizzard rages outside and the composer, lyricist, director and actors prepare for their performances, the Slasher reappears, striking again — and again, and again!

Assassins stalk each other through secret passageways and behind hidden library panels in an ever-increasing romp through comic pastiche involving German spies, a bumbling police investigator and a maid who is apparently four different people — all of which figure in the intrigue and hilarity before the Slasher is finally unmasked!

"The fun manages to be almost as plentiful as the bodies."
Evening Standard

"Imagine a 42nd Street with corpses where the songs ought to be."
Punch

"The effect is phenomenal and blinding — Take Shades." *Observer*

For further information contact Warner Chappell Plays Ltd, 129 Park Street, London WlY 3FA. Telephone 01-629-7600.